Praise for T

"Matthew West has a heart for message, music, and ministry. The three passions combine to create a wonderful outcome. Matthew has touched hearts around the globe, including mine, for decades. I'm excited about this book. I'm even more excited about Matthew and his life."

MAX LUCADO | PASTOR, SPEAKER, AND BESTSELLING AUTHOR
OF *HELP IS HERE* AND *YOU WERE MADE FOR THIS MOMENT*

"In his new book, *The God Who Stays*, Matthew West uses his personal story of trusting Jesus in difficult times to lift us up and deepen our faith. When everyone else turns away, when division and destruction and duplicity mark our culture, we are in dire need of this beautiful message. Turn off the TV and read this book!"

KAREN KINGSBURY | *NEW YORK TIMES* BESTSELLING AUTHOR

"I don't know the exact details of hard days you've lived through, but I know this: your story isn't over, and God is better than you can imagine. This has been true in my life, and my friend Matthew West shares his own journey, calling us back to the simplicity of walking with Jesus in the hard times and in the good ones. Matthew reminds us that faith is about trusting the God who is constantly pursuing and loving us."

CANDACE CAMERON BURE | ACTRESS, PRODUCER,
NEW YORK TIMES BESTSELLING AUTHOR

"Matthew has an incredible ability to impact lives and inspire others through his words and music. *The God Who Stays* reminds us that God will travel with us forever through our lives, no matter what. I believe this book will be an encouragement to everyone who reads it."

TIM TEBOW | *NEW YORK TIMES* BESTSELLING
AUTHOR, FORMER NFL QUARTERBACK

"Turbulent, unsteady, chaotic, and confused: these are the words I'd use to describe the current state of our world. And yet, in the face of the instability of our culture or of our own lives, God calls us to peace by reminding us of His steadfast presence. When everything's changing, when nothing is sure, when the very ground beneath us seems to be shifting under our feet, God promises that He will remain the same and He will stay with us. What sweet relief. *The God Who Stays* is a compelling and uplifting reminder of the only thing keeping us grounded in an age of anxiety and fear: God's unwavering faithfulness."

ALLIE BETH STUCKEY | COMMENTATOR, PODCAST HOST, AND
AUTHOR OF *YOU'RE NOT ENOUGH (AND THAT'S OKAY)*

"There are times in our lives when we feel desperate, alone, and without hope. We all feel that way during those difficult periods where hope can't be found. Matthew West is a voice that breaks through the darkness. His love for the Lord is contagious, and *The God Who Stays* will remind you that God will see you through. Throughout scripture there are countless examples of how God reminds His overwhelmed faithful that 'I will be with you.' This book will be a wonderful reminder that the God who stays will be by your side through every storm."

SCOTT HAMILTON | OLYMPIC FIGURE SKATING GOLD MEDALIST
AND *NEW YORK TIMES* BESTSELLING AUTHOR OF *FINISH FIRST*

"There are times when we feel desperate, alone, and without hope. Matthew West has a voice that breaks through the darkness. His new book, *The God Who Stays*, is a wonderful reminder that the One who never leaves us will stay by your side through every storm."

KIRK CAMERON | ACTOR AND FILMMAKER

"Matthew's passion for ministry, coupled with his gift for storytelling, has impacted people all over the world, including me. I am excited this new book will reach even more people. It is a must read! I will be sharing it with everyone I know!"

JON GORDON | 12X BESTSELLING AUTHOR OF
THE CARPENTER AND *THE GARDEN*

"In the midst of navigating the chaos of today's world, *The God Who Stays* reminds us of the truth of God's character. Matthew takes us back to who God is and the hope we can find in Him. He is a God who is with us in the highs and the lows. He doesn't pick and choose who He wants to comfort. When we seek first the Kingdom, nothing can separate us from God's love and kindness."

MADISON PREWETT | *THE BACHELOR* FINALIST
AND AUTHOR OF *MADE FOR THIS MOMENT*

"Matthew West is one of the most encouraging, kind-hearted, uplifting people I've ever met. We're neighbors. (Sort of.) Everyone who lives in Nashville are neighbors. But that's what this book felt like, a conversation with a neighbor who makes you laugh, think, and return to what matters most. If you need a reminder about what it really takes to get through a storm, look no further."

JON ACUFF | *NEW YORK TIMES* BESTSELLING AUTHOR OF
SOUNDTRACKS: THE SURPRISING SOLUTION TO OVERTHINKING

"This is the book we all need right now. And Matthew is the perfect person to write it."

"No matter who you are or where you are from, God has a plan for your life. *The God Who Stays* will help you learn to trust in His plan even when you can't see it. Matthew reminds you that God is actually the author of your story, so there's no need to worry. Let go, let God, and let Matthew be your guide on your journey to finding your true purpose."

"Matthew West is consistently encouraging—through his songwriting, his concerts, his podcast, and now in new and really profound ways through *The God Who Stays*. This book will journey with you, help you, and challenge you as you process the last few years and find God in the everyday experiences and the extraordinary ones too."

The God Who Stays

LIFE LOOKS DIFFERENT WITH HIM BY YOUR SIDE

Matthew West

with Matt Litton

W PUBLISHING GROUP

AN IMPRINT OF THOMAS NELSON

Published in Nashville, Tennessee, by W Publishing, an imprint of Thomas Nelson.

Thomas Nelson titles may be purchased in bulk for educational, business, fundraising, or sales promotional use. For information, please email SpecialMarkets@ThomasNelson.com.

Lyrics for "The God Who Stays" are used by permission of A. J. Pruis, Matthew West, and Jonathan Smith.

Lyrics for "Wonderful Life" are used by permission of A. J. Pruis and Matthew West.

Lyrics for "Take Heart" are used by permission of A. J. Pruis and Matthew West.

Unless otherwise noted, Scripture quotations are taken from The Holy Bible, New International Version®, NIV®. Copyright © 1973, 1978, 1984, 2011 by Biblica, Inc.® Used by permission of Zondervan. All rights reserved worldwide. www.zondervan.com. The "NIV" and "New International Version" are trademarks registered in the United States Patent and Trademark Office by Biblica, Inc.®

Scripture quotations marked MSG are taken from THE MESSAGE. Copyright © 1993, 2002, 2018 by Eugene H. Peterson. Used by permission of NavPress, represented by Tyndale House Publishers, a Division of Tyndale House Ministries. All rights reserved.

ISBN 978-0-7852-9164-0 (audiobook)
ISBN 978-0-7852-9163-3 (eBook)
ISBN 978-0-7852-9162-6 (TP)

Library of Congress Control Number: 2022005764

Printed in the United States of America

22 23 24 25 26   LSC   10 9 8 7 6 5 4 3 2 1

To my girls.

Contents

Foreword

When life takes unexpected turns or devastates us completely, we often think, *Where is God? Why can't I see Him move or feel Him with me?* In my own world, when God allows circumstances that deviate from the plan I'm assuming my life should follow, I'm much more likely to try to give Him a long list of all my suggestions for how a good God should surely fix this, rather than just listening for His instruction and trusting Him.

Maybe you do this too. And that's why this message is so valuable and timely for us.

Knowing and learning to trust the God who stays has been one of the most important aspects of my faith story. Through every season of my life, He's the One who has never left my side when loss shattered my heart to dust, when those I've counted on most have walked away, and when disappointments and disillusionments were all I could see.

In the pages that follow, Matthew's words will speak directly to you, even if your experiences don't mirror my own. Because we all need some help to more fully understand: *God is good. God is good to us. God is good at being God.*

Most days, we try our best to cling to the promises of God even though our difficult circumstances are shouting loudly, daring us to doubt His presence, goodness, and love. In these moments, we're tempted to label God as distant, unseeing, or even absent. But even though we have our doubts, God never wavers in being as trustworthy and present as He says He is.

He promises to stay when we're at our absolute worst.

He promises to stay when we're happy and celebrating a victory.

He promises to stay when we're broken or humiliated.

He promises to stay when life turns upside down.

He promises to stay when we're faithless.

And . . . He promises to stay when others walk away.

Fear, doubt, pain, and feeling overwhelmed often make us forgetful, which is why it's so crucial for us to look into God's Word so we can trace His hand of faithfulness in our lives and the lives of His people before us. Their struggles and hurts are no different than ours, and we have the same trustworthy and faithful God for our journey.

The God Who Stays is the book our aching and anxious souls have been waiting for. It's for all of us who are long overdue in taking the time to have a marked moment to pause and remember Immanuel—"God with us"—so we can move forward with hope. These teachings, along with the generous glimpse Matthew gives us into his faith walk, will help us find our footing in ours.

My prayer for us is that in reading this book, our faith in our ever-present and loving God will be reinvigorated. God isn't hiding from us. He's waiting to be seen by us. God isn't being silent. He's waiting for us to recognize His answers. God hasn't forgotten us. He's waiting for us to remember His goodness and faithfulness. And I'm so grateful to have a friend like Matthew to show us how he's done this and encourage us that we can too.

Much love from me to you, friend.

—*Lysa TerKeurst*

CHAPTER 1

Does God Keep His Distance?

Six Feet of Separation

New Year's always begins with such promise, doesn't it? Hope somehow feels a little closer that time of year. It certainly did on January 1 of 2020. I still recall laughing at how many pastors of churches across the country were inspiring their congregations with the exact same cleverly titled sermon theme: "20/20 Vision!" It was the beginning of a new decade. I remember hearing references to the "Roaring Twenties" in the media. It was a fresh start. Another new beginning. A clean slate and a blank calendar with plenty of open space for optimism. Oh, and I also *clearly* remember watching the ball drop on television, putting my arm around my wife, and uttering the following phrase:

"Honey, I've got a *really* good feeling about 2020 . . ."

Are you cringing just thinking of it now? Can you remember what you were doing at the beginning of that year? Did you have dreams? How about your carefully thought-out plans? What were your New Year's resolutions?

I had new music and a brand-new tour about to begin. I'd even titled my record *Brand New* because it was going to release in the early months of that super-promising year of our Lord, 2020. In early February, I traveled to New York City for some interviews and performances to promote the new record. It's one of my favorite places to visit. I brought my wife, Emily, along, and after my work was done promoting the record, we crowded into a tiny Italian joint for a quintessential Big Apple dining experience a few blocks from the theater where we had just seen *Hamilton*. Shoulder to shoulder, locals and tourists stuffed their faces with some of the best pasta outside of Italy. The energy was high; the volume level even higher. As we walked the city that night, we saw crowds everywhere. It was an amazing trip!

Just a few weeks later, I was back in the Big Apple as the wheels seemed to be rapidly coming off of . . . well . . . the entire world. It was mid-March by then and everyone was being thrown into a state of fear and uncertainty. As I rode through New York City on my way to New Jersey, the area reminded me of a ghost town or something from a science fiction movie. The streets of Manhattan that were vibrant and alive on my recent visit were as empty as the toilet paper aisle at my local Walmart. Remember how quickly it all happened? Do you recall the confusion and the uncertainty of that strange time? It seemed that this new mandate for the world to stay "six feet apart" was being preached in every broadcast, every news conference, and every conversation.

It was March 12, and I was planning to hit the stage in a Trenton, New Jersey, arena, just like sports teams and musicians and entertainers were still doing all over the country. I was sitting on the steps of the stage preparing for sound check, surrounded by mics, amps, instruments, and that important blue couch I'd brought on tour (more on that later). And that was the moment—as I was preparing to perform—we received word that the city of Trenton was shutting down and our show was canceled effective immediately. I sat there scrolling Twitter and watched as dozens of live events across America were also being shut down simultaneously in real time. The world was changing rapidly, and before we left the arena that day, the remainder of the tour had been canceled. I didn't understand it in the moment, but we were entering into a wilderness season. A time of exile from normal life.

I booked the last flight out that evening from the Philadelphia airport and called an Uber. I hurriedly packed my bags and hopped into a stranger's car. I wanted to get home to my family. The hour-long ride gave me time to try to process what was happening. Like everyone else, I was consumed with fear and worry: *My tour is canceled. People are depending on me. My family is depending on me. Is my career over? Is my family going to be safe? I just shook hands with thousands of people across multiple states on tour. What if I get sick? What if I spread it to my family?*

I know those days may still be uncomfortable to read about, like revisiting a bad movie. And I am painfully aware that so many people in the world faced much bigger questions and more terrifying challenges in those days. During that car ride, I began feeling utterly hopeless about a world that was spinning out of control.

And just then, something funny happened that snapped me out of my anxieties and brought me back to my seat in that Uber. The driver's radio was tuned in to a Christian music station and he began to passionately sing along to a song. The funny thing is, it was my song: "The God Who Stays." I leaned in from the back seat, highly entertained as I listened to my driver belt out the lyrics to my song in broken English:

> *You're the God who stays, You're the God who stays*
> *You're the One who runs in my direction*
> *When the whole world walks away*
> *You're the God who stands with wide open arms*
> *And you tell me nothing I have ever done can separate my heart*
> *From the God who stays*

I started to sing along with the driver, purposefully getting louder and louder, line by line thinking he might recognize the familiar voice. I shouted jokingly, "So . . . how do you think I sound?"

"Not so good," he said looking back at me in his rearview mirror.

I responded, "Yeah, I guess I don't sing quite as good as that guy on the radio, huh?"

"Not quite," he said, as he shook his head smiling. "But it's not your fault. You know, that guy does that for a living. You don't do that full-time. So, you are pretty good, but not so good. You keep trying!"

I laughed, enjoying the moment, and said, "Yeah, I guess you're right."

My driver's name was Arthur. He told me he loved that song on the radio and why it meant so much to him. He said he needed the reminder that God has stayed with him through everything: through his immigration to the United States, his separation from his family back home, his struggle to make enough money to survive and begin a new life.

It hit me that he sang that song as if he knew that God had surely stayed with him. As the entire world seemed to be falling apart, it was difficult to see where God was at the moment or how He was staying with us. As Arthur dropped me off and I sat on a half-empty plane with a mask on for the first time, I thought about that thirteen-year-old preacher's kid who believed he would get to heaven simply because he had the right family connections. The one whose parents always told him, "Matthew, Jesus loves you. He wants to have a personal relationship with you." That kid who came home after school one day, dropped his backpack at the front door, grabbed a snack, and plopped down on the blue couch in the basement of his childhood home, hoping to catch a Cubs game. Instead of baseball that afternoon, I found Billy Graham on the TV station preaching to a crowded stadium. And he was preaching to me. My heart received those words like a hard rain on a dry ground: "God loves you. He

5

sent His only Son to die on a cross for you to pay the price for your sins. God has a great plan for your life. Will you say yes to Him today?" I did. And from then on whenever I thought of the presence of God, I thought about that blue couch. It has been my reminder that God is close. And I thought it could be a reminder for others too. That's why I would bring a replica of the blue couch on stage with me. I'd tell my "blue couch story" every night in the hopes that people would discover that God is available to them too. However, that blue couch was about to be packed away for a long time. And that flight back to Nashville would be my last one for a while. God certainly didn't feel close with everything going on in the world around me.

The tour had ended abruptly, and my entire life was put on hold as we all watched, from our television screens, the world literally come to a standstill. My replica blue couch was sitting in a pay-by-the-month storage unit south of Nashville, gathering dust next to guitars and keyboards that were supposed to be making music on a stage somewhere in America. As I settled into a new normal of stay-at-home orders and masks and isolation, I felt a million miles away from that kid on the blue couch. The kid who couldn't deny that God was real, God loved him, and God would always be with him was now wondering if God Himself had chosen to social distance from the world for a while.

In the quiet of lockdown, it was apparent to me that my most passionate displays of faith usually took place when my faith was on display in front of a crowd. With no one to sing to, it dawned on me how I am good at declaring God's love in front of a crowd—I've perfected the art of speaking publicly about the grace of a Savior who can change someone's life; I know all the right scriptures, all the right words. I can look the part, even when I don't feel the part. And now I was stuck in the wilderness. In a season where God felt very distant, not just to me but for so many people in the world.

My public faith was on pause. My music ministry wasn't going anywhere for a while. The blue couch that represented the presence of God to me sat locked away in a storage unit and I sat in my home in Nashville, wondering what God was doing, where He was in all this hurt happening in the world, and impatiently waiting for life to begin again. Meanwhile, people lost their livelihoods and their lives, and social and political unrest was a daily reality. I began to understand that I probably wasn't the only person feeling like God had adopted His own social distance policy.

But I kept thinking about Arthur and the Uber ride to the airport and how he sang my song to me. I couldn't get that moment out of my head. Was God trying to use my own words to tell me something? *You're the God who stays, you're the God who stays . . .* Did I really believe what I'd been singing on stage each night? Why did that blue couch matter so much to me? Was I bringing it on the road hoping to recapture something I'd lost along the way?

This unexpected pause button had been pressed, and through my desperation I sat down to write. As I did, I began to recognize a familiar whisper. It was similar to the psalms where David asked God the same question: "Where are you?" I could almost hear him saying, "Are You staying six feet away from me?" I

7

THE GOD WHO STAYS

began to pray and study in hopes of rediscovering God's promises. And as the pandemic raged outside the safety of my home, I began to hear Him speaking: "Immanuel, God with us."

It wasn't "Immanuel, God with us only when we're perfect." I didn't hear, "Immanuel, the God who visits me only once on the blue couch." Had I left God in a place just as I had left that blue couch in a storage unit? Could it be that all the while He's been pursuing a closeness with me that I'd simply ignored? How long had I been singing the songs but missing the message? Was He there with the people in the hospital? With the frontline workers? The protesters and policemen? Had He been with His people through the crazy times in history? What was He doing in this season of wilderness? Would He walk with us into an uncertain future?

The voice of Arthur the Uber driver's broken English singing my song kept ringing in my ears. He didn't know that night as he drove me to the airport that he was singing for me. As I heard Arthur's voice in my head, I swear I could see God running toward me with open arms like the prodigal's father who came running out to meet his long-lost son even "while he was still a long way off" (Luke 15:20). I may not have looked like it to the audience at my shows, but perhaps I had been a long way off too. I missed the promise of God's closeness. I had settled for a socially distant relationship with the One who is nearer than I dare to believe, closer than the air I breathe. Maybe I had been keeping six feet of separation from the God who loves me.

[CHAPTER 2]

Why Does God Stay?

Super Dad or Shark Bait?

I remember sitting down at my piano searching the keys like a prayer. For some reason I began playing one note on the piano, over and over. Nothing fancy. Nothing complicated. Just one note. *Don't overthink it,* I thought. *Just say something true.* I was searching for simple, longing for solid ground. From there, the words and music for a song called "The God Who Stays" were born. The song was written before the world had considered new realities like social distancing, masking up, or stay-in-place orders. It was a hymn about the deepest things I believe about God. I didn't realize it at the time, but more than any song I had ever written, those words came out of an aching to get back to the basics of my faith. What is the one chord that brings us all together as believers? What is the one note that everything else is built on? What is the truth of how God really works in our lives? Sometimes, I feel like I write the songs I need to hear the most. I just didn't realize how much I would need those words until later. It was a longing for simplicity that began with just me at my piano considering the depth of God's love for me.

You're the God who stays
You're the One who runs in my direction
when the whole world walks away

You know why that song stood out from all the others I had recently written? Every moment I had to myself those first weeks off the road, I was transported into the back seat of that New Jersey Uber again. And I thought a lot about the joy in my driver, Arthur's, heart: his enthusiasm for life, his effervescent love for people, and his passion to learn a second language so that he could talk about his faith. How beautiful was it that he used those car rides to share his testimony with the hundreds of people he drove around that big city each week? I had an instrument. He had a cab. We were doing the same work. How many people had he impacted by sharing God's love?

Every time I closed my eyes during those weeks, I heard Arthur's voice singing my very own song back to me:

You're the God who stands
With wide open arms

He knew the truth of the God who stays, and it radiated from his life. Isn't it amazing how God's most beautiful words can come to us in broken English? Isn't it something how God can use strangers to speak to us in a way that we can hear Him? I felt like God was whispering to me to come sit down and have a talk. I knew that meeting the cab driver who sang my own song back to me was no accident, just like turning on my TV to find Billy Graham preaching instead of my Cubs playing that long-ago day was no accident.

And now with the whole world put in time-out for a while, God had my full attention. It was hard to see where He was doing good as I scrolled the news apps on my phone or turned on the television. But as I turned my attention toward my own home, I was so grateful that my family was safe and healthy during a time when things were difficult for so many people. All the frivolity in life was tossed aside in that season. The entire West family—me; my wife, Emily; and our two daughters—were home with no school, no practices, no concerts, no church gatherings, *nothing* to do. Our world had come to a complete standstill. I didn't realize it at the time, but we were living the lines from Psalm 46:10: "Be still, and know that I am God." Exodus 14:14 summed it up as well: "The LORD will fight for you; you need only to be still." I'd read throughout the Bible that God does His best work when we are still—I guess if the psalmist could have written something for our current days it would've been, "Be *quarantined*, and know that I am God."

Back to the Blue Couch

The words to that song were swirling in my head and calling me back to a spiritual simplicity that I needed. I wanted the intimacy with God that I'd somehow lost. The closeness with Jesus I'd found on the blue couch and in a Billy Graham sermon. That moment that first showed me how much God loved me. I had embraced the John 3:16-ness of the good news in my parents' basement that day, and it changed my life forever: "For God so loved the world that he gave his one and only Son, that whoever believes in him shall not perish but have eternal life." That was the moment when God's love was just . . . simple. I didn't know much back then; I just knew I needed Jesus and I dared to believe that He wanted to be with me.

Jesus *wanted* to be with me.

It's like He wanted me to get back to that one simple chord—that one everlasting truth. God was using this time to point out how I had been keeping Him at arm's length. I was beginning to realize that I had been missing all the notes that fill out the depth of God's love. I had proclaimed the truth from stages with excitement and passion but wasn't really experiencing it in my personal life. I'd been living like a fitness trainer who couldn't do a push-up. A chef who couldn't scramble an egg. A musician who couldn't play an instrument. I intellectually knew that God loved me, but my heart was missing the song—I had all the information memorized, but I was missing the relationship. Maybe you've been there, too, at different times in your walk with God. Maybe you are there today.

It can be easy to forget the depth of God's love. Sometimes we get wrapped up in the God-approval game. After all, the whole world is focused on what we can earn, what we accomplish, or what we "deserve," and it is easy to forget God doesn't work that way. God loves us just as we are—not for what we do. I needed that reminder. Just like when I sat down at that piano in my studio, I wanted to rediscover the notes that made up the profound chord of God's eternal love for me. I felt like God was wanting to remind me not just that He stays with me, but *why* He stays.

A Walk in the Garden

Getting back to the basics for me begins with getting back to the Bible, so I turned to the first chapters of Genesis to read God's love letter to the world. I guess I wanted to start at the creation story where everything was good just as God had intended it to be. And that is when I noticed something beautiful about God and His relationship with His people. The Bible says in Genesis 3:8 that God "was walking in the garden in the cool of the day" right before Adam and Eve heard Him coming and ran away to hide. Something captured my heart in that simple line. I sat back and thought about God taking a walk through the garden. It isn't a verse that I hear preached often, but it caught my attention and I read it again. The Bible doesn't say God was out for a walk in the garden for the first time ever. And Adam and Eve didn't seem the least bit surprised to hear God a few steps away when they ran and hid from Him. No, as I read it again, it seemed apparent that God had a habit of taking walks in the garden with Adam and Eve, and maybe it was even a daily thing. It made me remember "In the Garden," one of the many old hymnal songs that helped me fall in love with gospel music: "And He walks with me, and He talks with me, and He tells me I am His own . . ."[1]

Consider for a minute that the God of the universe, the Alpha and Omega, the Beginning and the End, came to the garden He created to walk and talk with Adam and Eve. For some reason, that idea made me sit back and think about God's love from a different perspective. It made me think about the people in my life who I go on walks with. They're the people I want to spend time with the most. I think about my walks with Emily. We don't just walk to make sure we get our ten thousand steps in; we talk about life, we work out problems, we communicate. We connect. There's something beautifully personal about taking a walk with someone.

There Is "Like" in the Love

When I was starting out in Nashville, I knocked on doors and sent demos all over town. I'd play or sing anywhere I had the opportunity. I was also getting one rejection after another after another, until finally I received a call from a label that asked me to come in and play a few songs for their team. It was the only label that hadn't yet turned me down. I was getting work as a songwriter behind the scenes, writing songs for others to record.

But I was beginning to wonder if a record deal of my own just wasn't part of God's plan. I showed up with my guitar and the little hope I still had, prepared to play music and meet the record label's team. I had my game face on. I was focused. I was ready. I had one goal that day: knock 'em off their feet. I didn't expect to be knocked off of my feet!

Amid some suits and ties in the audience of executives was a drop-dead gorgeous marketing manager. *Stay focused, West,* I thought as I strummed the first chords of my opening song. *You're here to get a record deal, not a wife!* After my audition, she approached me and struck up a conversation. She asked me to hang out a few times—a cookout at the house of the president of the record label, a country music concert at the stadium downtown, stuff like that. The entire time we hung out, I thought it was part of her job description to introduce new artists to the music industry or something. Not once did it dawn on me that we might be on an actual date! There was just no way! She was beautiful and successful. I was an unknown singer with a bad haircut (think '90s boy-band frosted tips). One night, we went for a walk in downtown Franklin, Tennessee, where the conversation was about much more than the music business. We talked about life, our previous relationships; she shared about a recent breakup. She even told me what kind of dog she always wanted and what she would name it someday: a pug named "Earl."

As I drove her home that night after our walk, I said, "Emily, I think you're really great. And you've been so kind to show me around town. I hope you find someone who really deserves you."

There was a long, awkward silence until she said through a

smile, "Matthew, what are you talking about? I *really* like spending time with you." My expression must've indicated I wasn't getting the picture, so she reiterated, "I *really* like you."

I was stunned. I explained, "I thought being nice to me was part of your job!"

We still laugh about that moment to this day! But I'll never forget that feeling. It was way better than any record deal. I mean, I really liked her. So, not only did I get signed by a record label from that one day playing music, but I also met my wife. I always remember how my heart felt when I heard the girl who I thought was way out of my league say, "I like you." I guess a big part of our love was the like. As in: I *liked* to hear her talk, I *liked* being with her, I *liked* her smile, I *liked* going on walks with her . . . and I am thankful that she still feels the same about me after almost twenty years of marriage! I think if love is a chord, then *like* would be one of the notes.

We *like* the people we love—and so does God. Something about that image of God walking with Adam and Eve in the garden helped me understand how powerful it is that God actually *likes* to be with us. Maybe we forget that simple note underneath the reality that God loves us—He *really* likes us! Sometimes I think it's hard for us to believe that God likes us, especially when we are having a really hard time liking ourselves. He truly likes who we are: He likes to hear us talk. He likes to see us smile. He likes to hear us laugh. He likes to be with us.

And because He liked being with them, God came walking "in the cool of the day" toward Adam and Eve. He was on His way to see them! The Bible doesn't say they were out walking toward God. He was definitely moving toward them. When you look through the Bible, it seems that in every story—from creation to Abraham on a mountain to Moses and a burning bush to Elijah after the storm to Mary and Joseph in a dream—from the very beginning of time God has always been the One coming toward us. And God went to the most extreme lengths to send His Son. I've always loved how *The Message* version of John 1:14 describes Jesus as God moving into the neighborhood. God seeks us out! Francis Thompson talks about God's relentless pursuit of humans in his poem "The Hound of Heaven," a concept further explored by J. R. R. Tolkien, G. K. Chesterton, and C. S. Lewis.

It's another note in that beautiful chord of God's love for us. He pursues us. Not only does God like our company, but He will also do *anything* to be with us. And that made me think about the people who I really want to spend time with—so much so that I would go to crazy lengths to be with them. Even if it meant facing one of my deepest childhood fears.

Swimming with the Sharks

I love my mom and dad and they were good parents with one small exception: they let me watch the movie *Jaws* when I was young. For this reason, I grew up with an irrational fear of sharks. I know it's strange for a Chicago kid, a thousand miles from the nearest ocean, to worry about sharks. But I vividly remember, as a nine-year-old, getting spooked while I was in the swimming pool in my friend's backyard. It's like I could hear that hauntingly famous John Williams tuba music beginning to play slowly when I went underwater, and I imagined a shark could somehow travel thousands of miles over concrete to get into that pool with me. (Don't judge. I know there are people who had that same fear!) I grew out of that and can swim fearlessly in suburban pools now, but I am still afraid of sharks. Needless to say, you know what isn't on my bucket list? Swimming with them.

Fast-forward to being the dad of a teenage daughter. If you've read the Bible story of Daniel and the lions' den, well, I may have a newer version of that story we could call "Matthew and the Bull Shark Reef." But it is also a story that taught me a lot about how far we will go to be with the people we love. My oldest daughter, Lulu, was about to have a big birthday. We go all out for birthdays in our house—I'll tell you more about that later. But this was her thirteenth and I wanted it to be really special. Lulu has always wanted me to watch Shark Week with her and she is super adventurous. So, I should've seen it coming when we were sitting around the dinner table, and I told her that I wanted to take her on a weekend trip to celebrate her birthday.

She began to talk through some ideas but then quickly landed on sharks. "Dad, I'd really love to go someplace like South Africa and swim with great white sharks, but maybe we could just find a place in Florida to do it?" I laughed to myself and thought, with all the confidence in the world, that we would *never* find a place in America that would let civilians do something so dangerous. Of course, Siri and Alexa and Google were all conveniently available to ruin any chance I had to get out of shark-diving. I was able to surprise Lulu by finding a shark cage–diving expedition off the coast of Florida. I booked flights, hotels, and reservations. Being lowered into the water with sharks didn't sound like my idea of a great time, but I *really* wanted to spend time with my daughter. And how dangerous could it really be? We were going to be inside a protective cage, right?

A few weeks later, I found myself two miles off the coast of Florida on a small boat with a captain, his young assistant, and a few other brave divers. I was a little nervous, but Lulu was so excited, and I was locked in to being Super Dad for the day. It didn't help calm my nerves that the captain of our little vessel looked just like the one from the first *Jaws* movie (and he smelled like last night's bottle of scotch too). Fortunately, there was a large, sturdy-looking cage standing at the back of the boat, as was promised on the website. I was able to stay calm, collected, and even felt a little confident about going underwater with some strong metal bars between me and a shark. We had dropped anchor and the young assistant began to free dive into the water with crates full of cut-up fish. He was "chumming the water." After submerging several times, he swam up and yelled, "We have bull sharks!" He paused to catch his breath. "There's about *twenty* of them down there!" Lulu's face broke into a huge smile. Some other people on the boat clapped nervously. I, on the other hand, was discovering the real reason why they call the outfit I was zipping up a "wet suit."

I've watched enough Shark Week shows to know all about bull sharks. They are aggressive and unpredictable. I also happen to know that a real live bull shark was probably the inspiration for the movie *Jaws*. *At least we have a cage!* I thought to myself. Just as I was clinging for dear life to that small comfort, the captain walked back and threw out a rope that floated forty feet behind the boat. He turned to us and joyously explained, "The water is great today, folks, so we are going to go outside of the cage and swim with the sharks in open water." Lulu might have giggled with excitement, but all I could hear were those words still hanging in the air making all my dad-alarms go off: "*outside of the cage.*"

Six brave, cageless souls climbed into an ocean full of bull sharks with only two clear instructions from the captain: First, we should always keep our eyes on the sharks. (Reassuring, right?) And second, because we were in the open sea and could easily be carried too far from the boat by the current, we should *never, ever* let go of the rope. Minutes into this adventure, I looked around and realized that Lulu had somehow become separated from me and was farther out on the line away from the boat. All my dad instincts kicked in. I knew there were twenty unpredictable sharks under us, and my daughter was not within my reach. There was no way I was going to be separated from her! Nothing was going to happen to her on my watch.

I transformed into Super Dad. I began to slowly work my way down the rope from the boat. But my hands slipped and the next thing I knew I was drifting underwater away from everyone. The captain told us to never let go of the rope! I looked down at the sharks swimming below me. I didn't even need the *Jaws* music. I panicked like that kid in a suburban Chicago pool and reached for anything I could to secure myself from drifting away. In one slip, I had transformed from Super Dad to Shark Bait. In my frantic grasping, I found *something* to hold on to . . . well, *someone.* I was safe! But as I stopped panicking, I realized that I was now holding on for dear life to the grown man who had been snorkeling next to me. My hands were securely around his waist and my face was pressed firmly against the backside of his wet suit. To make matters worse, he began to panic because I was pulling him underwater. "What in the world are you doing?" he shouted. Holding on to his waist for dear life, all I could say was, "I'm so sorry!" I am happy to tell you that the only part of me that I lost while shark diving on the open sea was my dignity.

I laugh now about my diving adventure as I consider my heavenly Father's love. I reflect on that trip and the message that I hope it communicated to my Lulu. I want to be with her so much that I would even willingly swim with sharks. I hope she remembers that truth for her whole life. I wasn't out there thrill-seeking. I was there because I love her, but also because I love being with her. And I will never forget the urgency I felt when we were separated in the ocean. Honestly, nothing was going to keep me from getting to Lulu. Maybe that's the same kind of urgency God feels when you or I begin to drift away from Him. I think God is in Super Dad mode all the time. And that is another note in the chord of God's love. He will go anywhere and cover any distance to be with you.

Is There Time for Me in God's Busy Schedule?

I've thought recently about how I can easily get so busy running from one meeting to the next, one concert to the next, one songwriting session to the next that I just don't feel like I have time for people. It seems like being busy is a badge of honor in our current world. Like busyness somehow makes us more important. And while I am thankful to be busy, I also think about the times when my to-do lists get in the way of being with the people I love. If we value our relationships, we must work to make them a priority. I didn't consider it at first, but God's taking the time to walk in the garden demonstrated that kind of commitment. If you think your day is busy, imagine God's schedule. I'm sure He has a lot going on managing the universe. But in that Genesis verse, God was walking to see Adam and Eve like it was a priority to Him.

My dad makes it a priority to come over to my studio each week to help me host a virtual devotional called 'Quiet Time' on my social media channels. He also makes guest appearances on my podcast and often goes on tour with me. He has always been more than just my dad; he is also my pastor. People ask me from time to time if growing up as a preacher's kid was tough on me. While being part of the family forever seated in the front-row pew every Sunday came with its challenges, my dad always made me feel important. No matter what he had going on with his work and ministry, he was never too busy to be my dad. But he was like that with everyone. And I think that taught me a lot about God's commitment to me.

I remember being jealous about how much my friends wanted to hang out with my dad when I was growing up. Sometimes, it could even get a little annoying because I would wonder if my buddies were coming over to hang out with me or my dad. But I didn't realize at the time how unusual it was to have a dad who really made me a priority. He made all my friends feel the same way. It was like they had a second dad. Looking back on those days, I realize that a lot of my buddies were about to become products of broken homes. A lot of them were dealing with some tough issues in their lives. What they weren't getting at home, they were getting from my dad, and I didn't even realize it.

Dad is fun to be around, but that wasn't why my friends loved him so much. They simply knew that he wanted to spend time with them. If you were with Dad, he was with you. You had his full attention. What a legacy he has cultivated by simply making people a priority. There was nothing so important in his life that if someone needed him, Dad wouldn't drop everything to be with them. Just like he'd drop everything to be with me. The truth is that God is the exact same way with us. There is simply nothing on God's schedule or agenda that ever takes precedence over spending time with me. Isn't that something to consider?

One time a young man named Aiden called in to my podcast from Canada. He was in the sixth grade, and he had tons of positive energy. He said, "Matthew West, God is so good to me!" He had started five businesses and was excited to talk about how God had gifted him to be a graphic designer—and he was only in the sixth grade! He had an enthusiasm and excitement about life. The last thing he said made me laugh because it was odd but very appropriate to the conversation I had been having with God lately. He said, "God is *so* good that He would take the time out of His schedule to love us." That statement from a young kid reminded me there is nothing more important to God than being with me. Of course, God stays because you and I are a priority to Him. What an incredible truth! It's like the last note in that chord of God's love for us.

He Walks with Me and Talks with Me

During the season of being quarantined at home, we began to spend a lot more time together as a family. As God continued to remind me of why He promises to stay with me, I kept think-ing about those walks in the garden from the story of Genesis. I thought each day about the reality that walks are what you do with people you love. I was learning that God didn't just love me and He wasn't distant; He was right there and *wanting* to spend time with me. My family started an evening tradition during lockdown, one that we still do today. Every evening we began to go on a family walk to get outside in the fresh air and just enjoy each other's company. Those walks are one of the gifts we have held on to from that hard season of life. It's become a way for me to unplug and catch up with Emily and the girls.

The weather on our evening walks doesn't always qualify as the "cool of the day" here in Tennessee. More like, "in the sweat-drenched humidity of the South." But I wouldn't miss those walks with my family for anything. I love being with them. I love to hear what they have to say. I really love talking to them about their day. I love listening to what they are learning. I love seeing them grow and change. I love those moments where there is nothing but us. And often now, those moments together make me think about what it must have been like for Adam and Eve to go on walks with God in the garden. Did they go every evening? Did God ask them about their day? Did He want to know what they thought of this or that? I bet He did.

I think if we just pay closer attention, God is like that with us. I remember another old hymn we used to sing in Dad's church growing up called "I Serve a Risen Savior" by A. H. Ackley—more popularly known as "He Lives"—about how Jesus walks and talks with us throughout our life journeys. Maybe getting back to the truth of the God who stays was just that easy. Maybe rediscovering that one chord that matters, the intimacy with God I was missing, begins with accepting that God doesn't just love me, He really *likes* me. I want to believe He comes to us every day the same way He did to Adam and Eve. I think we are a priority to Him. He likes the way you talk and sing and laugh and cry. He likes your smile. He likes your company. I believe He really likes you. Maybe that is one chord that brings us all together as believers—the notes on which we can build our lives.

[CHAPTER 3]

God Stays with His Plan

Minor League Dreams vs. Major League Plans

I'm just old enough to remember the days when you needed a paper map to get to places you'd never been before. I remember those first road trips I took from Chicago to Nashville when there was no such thing as Google Maps, Waze, or GPS. I used to roll my eyes when parents started a sentence with the words, "Back in my day . . ." As in, "Back in my day we had to walk through a foot of snow just to get to school. And it was uphill both ways!" Well, I can't believe I'm actually about to say this, but back in my day, we didn't get a heads-up about future traffic jams. Bumper-to-bumper traffic was just a fun surprise! We didn't have a voice telling us that there were "hazards reported ahead," and we could easily speed past a police car, resulting in a ticket. We didn't even know ahead of time if a road was closed; we just enjoyed taking a scenic route off the interstate when it happened. Way back then, there were songs about how "life is a highway," and we knew what that meant because our road trips were real adventures and sometimes just as unpredictable as real life. These days I can't even imagine how I would get by without my navigation apps. As a musician, I've spent thousands of hours touring America on a bus each year and I've started to take for granted that we'll always know how and when we will get to our destinations. I guess most of the world has gotten used to relying on our "network connections" to show us the way.

Until they don't work, of course. Until something goes wrong, and our maps won't refresh. That is a pretty good metaphor for what happened to the entire world in early 2020, right? Talk about having a "Jesus, take the wheel" moment! We all had that big road trip called 2020 well-planned out—and then everything went sideways. There were no clear directions to get us out of that mess and no plans that weren't rerouted. I had all kinds of new dreams on my "road map," and I know you did too. We all went from a new year rolled out in front of us like an open road to being locked down. From on time to indefinitely delayed. My work was canceled and the very future of the music industry was in serious jeopardy. But as hopeless as all that sounds, I also understood that I was one of the fortunate ones to be able to say that I was with my family, healthy and safe at home.

Still, none of our plans seemed to work for our new situation. There was no navigation app for this. I felt completely lost, and it brought up some serious doubts for me about the "God who stays." Basic questions like, Is God still in control? Is He as surprised as we are at all of this? Was God watching our lives play out like some M. Night Shyamalan movie, saying to Himself, "Wow, I didn't see that one coming!" I remember hearing the same phrase from all the news reporters, that we were living in "unprecedented" times. I often thought, *When can we all just get back to some precedented times?* But I also knew from the Bible that even the wild days of pandemics and natural disasters were precedented.

I would often think about Jeremiah 29:11 because it is one of my favorite verses. "'For I know the plans I have for you,' declares the LORD, 'plans to prosper you and not to harm you, plans to give you hope and a future.'" It sounds upbeat because it is such a divine and hopeful promise. God has plans for you, and they are good. But as I went back and read that scripture in Jeremiah, I was reminded that the promise was spoken to Israel during their own "unprecedented" times. When the people of Israel first heard about this promise of God's plans, they were in exile, which is a nice way of saying they had been conquered by a brutal army and forced to move to another country to be slaves. Kind of makes a worldwide pandemic sound like a breeze. But right before that great promise, God also told them they needed to be prepared for seventy more years of slavery and oppression!

That kind of plan was hopeful and discouraging all at the same time. If I were an Israelite, I am sure I would have responded to God's promise in that famous verse with, "Lord, I love your idea about the plans to prosper me and give me a hope and a future. All that is so good. Now, if you can just change the part about seventy more years in slavery, I think we'll have a deal!"

Honestly, we don't have to look too far back to reveal tough times like we've endured recently. The reality is that difficult times have come and gone throughout history. As I've traveled the country, I've met the most amazing people, and I can tell you story after story of lost jobs, terminal diagnoses, grief, life-altering accidents, broken relationships, tragedies, and major setbacks that left good, faithful Jesus followers saying, "Lord, what in the world is the plan?" Times when the navigation apps for our lives no longer work. Honestly, these kinds of situations—whether they are personal, national, or global—leave us desperately searching for proof that God still stays with us in our lives.

What do we do when our plans have been sidetracked, derailed, or unraveled? Does God really factor things like a worldwide pandemic into His plans for us? Was God still in control in all this chaos? On top of everything going on in the world, what did God want me to do? Was He giving up on His original plan for me to play music? I remembered in the Bible when God's people were traveling through the wilderness, they would stop to build altars whenever He would do something for them. They weren't just building these to honor God. They were doing it to remember God's faithfulness! They built them so they would never forget that God had a plan.

I suddenly had a lot of time on my hands as I sat down to write to think back on my life. I thought about that last show I was able to play the evening before things shut down, and I wondered if God had plans to ever let me play in front of people again. Maybe I just needed to remember what God had already done in my life to bring me where He wanted me to be. I was missing the little things that had been taken from us during that time, like getting a decent haircut, going out to a restaurant, or seeing my Cubs play baseball. And that made me remember the early years of my walk with Jesus, right after that Billy Graham sermon had changed my life. I thought back to my thirteen-year-old self who had just started following Jesus, when I had a much different plan than God did. I realized that I had minor league dreams, but God had major league plans.

God's Plans Are Always Greater Than Ours

When I think back on my plans for my life now, they seem kind of silly. I can still remember sitting at my high school English teacher's desk while she lectured me about some of my missing homework. Let's just say I wasn't super concerned with my grades at that time in my life because I thought I had better options than school. She was worried about my performance in her class, and I was only half listening while I looked through my backpack for just the right folder. As she was still talking, I finally found it. *My* life plans! I opened the folder and slid an important piece of paper across the desk to her. I wish I could tell you that it was a missing homework assignment or one of those "write this life lesson one hundred times" apology letters that teachers used to make you do when you got in trouble at school—but it wasn't.

It was a newspaper clipping that I had cut out at home and always kept with me. It was a *Chicago Sun-Times* article that listed the best baseball players in the metropolitan area. I proudly pointed to the list, as if it were an excuse for my poor performance in her class, a counter to her argument that I needed to turn in my homework on time. You see, right there in that news clipping was yours truly, me, the one and only Matthew West, listed as the number one first baseman in the entire Chicago area. And at that point in my teenage life, it was all I thought I needed—because *baseball* was my plan. I suppose it's obvious how well that all worked out for me. I often say from the stage during my concerts, "I don't want to brag, but I was an incredible baseball player back in the day. In fact, I was such a great baseball player that now I stand up in front of people and play a guitar and sing for a living!" I thought I'd be swinging a baseball bat. God saw me strumming a guitar. I thought I'd have a glove in one hand and a ball in the other. God saw me with a pen and paper writing songs and books.

I was the boy who would watch Cubs games in my basement, dreaming about playing first base in those clean, white uniforms with the royal pinstripes at Wrigley Field. The reality is, the closest I've ever gotten to professional baseball is when I was invited to sing the national anthem for a Cubs game in 2015. As much as I'd like to think I had something to do with my Cubbies' 2–0 win against the Giants that day, I was watching the first pitch sitting in the stands of my favorite baseball stadium. And I think all Chicago fans should probably say a special thank-you to Jesus that I didn't play first base for the team. But isn't it funny to remember the things that we had planned for our lives and compare them to where we are now? I would never have imagined back then that I would grow up to play music as a job. And I bet you could have never convinced this pastor's kid that he would grow up and do ministry work!

God had a plan that was much bigger, bolder, and ultimately way better than mine. Sometimes the best things in life are the plans that don't work out. When people talk about the highlights of their lives, you'll often hear them refer to "the best thing that ever happened." As in, "Meeting my wife was the best thing that ever happened to me." But I can't help but think about the best things that *never* happened. I often talk about the dreams that don't come true for us and the fact that rejection is never really rejection when you know who the real Author of your story is. When everything seems like it is falling apart and all our plans are failing, it helps to look back and see that God doesn't waste His time with minor league directions; His destinations are always big league! In those moments when we see our plans falling apart, God sees His plan falling into place.

We Can't Always See God's Plan Coming Together

This time reflecting on my own story reminded me of how important it is to trust God. And trusting God when I can't see the plan has always been a big challenge for me. Maybe it is for you too. I am a self-diagnosed control freak, and I don't like it when I can't see where God is taking me. Maybe you can relate. One of the things I have noticed in the Bible is that God's people often lose sight of the truth that He always stays with His plan. In Exodus, when Moses was leading Israel out of slavery, God put on a shock-and-awe-level, big-budget-action-movie kind of miracle show. There were staffs turning into snakes, locust and frog infestations, a river turning to blood—and that was just the beginning! God parted a sea and drowned the best army on earth, and then He provided a pillar of fire at night and a cloud during the day to make sure His people didn't get lost in the wilderness.

All these huge miracles revealed to the Israelites that He intended to stay faithful to His plan. Yet they still kept forgetting to trust. Israel was just a few days removed from witnessing these miracles when they began to lose their cool with Moses because they thought he had led them out into the wilderness to starve. In fact, the Bible says they preferred to go back to Egypt! As crazy as that sounds, sometimes we can act the same way. I can see God move in a powerful way and then a week later question what He is doing. Perhaps it is human nature to lose trust that God has a plan. I found it helpful to spend time remembering and being grateful for how God has worked in my story. God was paving a way for a plan I couldn't see.

I wasn't a great student, and despite my newspaper shout-out for baseball, I never received a single scholarship offer. But God had a plan for me, according to the way He designed me, even if I couldn't see it. Interestingly, I never paid attention to how involved I was in singing as I was growing up. I sang in church. All the senior citizens at the retirement center we visited at Christmastime used to tell me I had a beautiful voice. I had the lead role in "The Sixth-Grade Scrooge," a critically acclaimed church musical performance. (Okay, maybe there wasn't so much critical acclaim.) Still, I was always a reluctant member of the choir. Mrs. Maholek wouldn't let me quit despite my best efforts. And when we put on chorus performances, I didn't practice the songs. I would just show up and sing.

I didn't consider music a part of the plan for me until I had to find a way to pay for college, and my choir teacher suggested that I audition for a scholarship in the school of music. For the audition, I was supposed to sing a classical piece. I arrived and sang the tenor part for Handel's *Messiah*; the catch was that I sang it like it was a Boyz II Men song! I was doing it R&B style, and all the classical music professors looked at me a little confused and concerned. When I was done, they asked, "So, you like pop music, right?" I was sure it didn't go well and that there was no way I was going to get the scholarship. But God had a different plan. They somehow liked what they heard, and I guess they thought I had potential. Talk about a miracle—I was offered a scholarship!

I spent a lot of time alone in my room my freshman year of college learning guitar chords and writing songs. Even though I wasn't a baseball player anymore, I did live in the same dorm as the athletes. I didn't really fit in with the kids in the music program because I wasn't a classical musician, and I didn't fit in with the athletes because I wasn't on a team. It was a lonely year. But my dorm room became my studio. After a few months, the guys in my dorm began to ask me if I would play songs for them out in the lobby. And then I started to receive invites to play my songs at fraternity events. I was as shocked as anyone that people started to show up to watch me play and sing. One of my favorite music professors even teased me about my songwriting. He said, "You really love to write songs about the two Gs: God and girls." I've always remembered that comment because after all these years as a musician, it's still true! I still find myself writing songs about God and songs about my three girls.

I was invited one night to play at a big party at the TKE house. Late that evening they cleared the dance floor and wanted me to come out with an acoustic guitar and play songs I had written about God. There in the dingy, beer-soaked basement of the frat house was the first time I truly realized what God was doing with music in my life. I was singing songs and ministering to people! Looking back on my life story, it is funny to see God's plan and how different it was from mine. I was a pastor's kid who never planned to go into ministry and dreamed only of playing baseball. And as clearly as I can see God's purpose and plan looking back now, there is no way I could've understood it as I was going through those experiences. We don't always see what God is doing behind the scenes of our lives. We just have to trust.

This truth washed over me as I sat alone writing in the Story House, wondering what would happen with a pandemic raging in the world outside my door and what God had next for me.

As Simple as the Next Right Thing

I thought about one of the heroes of the Bible who never seemed to know exactly what to do or what was going on in his life, yet he just kept being faithful by doing the next right thing. Joseph was thrown into a pit to die by his own brothers, but God used that moment to rescue him and take him to Egypt, where he gained power and influence. Though he ran into all kinds of trouble, he never lost hope. He just kept doing the next right thing. He was wrongfully accused and thrown in jail, but God used that situation to put him in a position to interpret dreams for the king. He gained favor with the king and was placed in charge of the entire kingdom.

Joseph went on to rescue all of Egypt from a famine. But the best part of the story is that those very brothers who left Joseph for dead came to Egypt during the famine looking for help, and they didn't even recognize him. God used Joseph to save his brothers and his father, the people who would become the nation of Israel. As you read the story of Joseph, you realize that there is no way he could have seen God's plan for his life as it was unfolding. He just showed up to each situation committed to being honest and faithful. God had designs and plans for Joseph to save his family the whole time!

Whenever I read that story, I wonder what God has in store for you and me that we just can't see. Maybe God wants us to keep doing the next right thing and rely on Him. And what if God has a plan for you, like He did for Joseph, to accomplish something that only you were designed to do?

Fingerprints, Brains, and the Walking Miracles We Are

Science backs up the truth that we are all uniquely made. I read an article recently that said every single human being on the planet has their own distinctive fingerprint that is completely unlike anyone else's. And scientists have also discovered that our brains are as unique as our fingerprints. Did you know that no two people in the whole world have the same brain anatomy? Explains a lot, right? We are wonderfully made. Just like King David wrote in Psalm 139, "For you created my inmost being; you knit me together in my mother's womb. I praise you because I am fearfully and wonderfully made; your works are wonderful, I know that full well" (vv. 13–14). If we are made that uniquely, then isn't it obvious that God would have a unique plan for each of our lives?

This makes me think of my buddy William. I met him before a show in New Mexico at a VIP meet and greet. In a line of about a hundred people, William walked up to me with a big smile on his face and said, "I heard you like stories . . . well, I'd like to tell you about my miracle." I could tell that he didn't have use of his left hand and that he had a slight limp when he walked. He struggled with his speech as well, but this thirteen-year-old was determined to tell me what God was doing in his life. After suffering a series of life-threatening strokes as an infant, the doctors had told his parents that he wouldn't make it, but he did. Then the doctors had told him he would never walk. They also said he wouldn't talk.

And now William is a high school student who uses his own

story to help and encourage people—and he sees it all as part of God's plan. Yes, those doctors told William he would never walk, but God had a different plan for his life, and one Easter Sunday after he gave his testimony, William dropped the microphone and ran a lap around the church auditorium. He told me he got a standing ovation from the church. How can you not cheer when you're witnessing firsthand evidence of God's faithfulness? He is such a remarkable kid that I always wonder what God has planned for him next. He was so inspiring to me that I had to write a song about him I called "Walking Miracles." William is like a modern-day Joseph story that is still unfolding in powerful ways. God made William like no one else to accomplish a plan that He had for no one else but William.

Sometimes I forget all too quickly what God has already done in my life when I come to a place where my plan doesn't seem to be working. Who was I to be so despondent about what was going on in the world after God had been so faithful to me? God's plan wasn't clear as the world was shutting down around us, but I look back on those quarantine days now and see how blessed I was that my family was protected. I couldn't see what God was doing. While I was busy wondering if I would ever play music again, God was bringing people into my life to start a podcast that would reach two million listeners for Christ. I also began a Wednesday devotional time that allowed me to encourage people every week, connect to their stories, and join them together in praying for one another's needs. I wrote a song about the pandemic that was a hit on YouTube and made people laugh and smile through some pretty difficult times. And I also

THE GOD WHO STAYS

began writing this book. Of course, none of these things were part of *my* original plan, and none of them could've happened without the rest of the world being put on hold. I didn't see any of this stuff on my road map. The most important part was that God used this unplanned wilderness time to show me why He stays with me. To remind me that even in the most confusing circumstances of life, He has a design and a path specifically for me.

Maybe God's Plan Is to Get Us Home to Him?

Long before Jeremiah was delivering important messages to the Israelites about God's plans for them, there was a powerful message delivered to Jeremiah about his own life. God said in Jeremiah 1:5, "Before I formed you in the womb I knew you, before you were born I set you apart; I appointed you as a prophet to the nations." So, before the world ever needed his words, God made it clear to Jeremiah that there was a plan and a purpose and a specific design for his life! How powerful is it to consider that when the world goes haywire, when all our direction apps fail, God is simply staying with His plan? And it isn't something He came up with on the fly. It was a plan designed before you were ever born!

Only when I take the time to look back over my own life, both the silly moments and the profound ones, can I see where God was working behind the scenes, through the people around me, in every circumstance—even a cab driver in New Jersey singing my song back to me. The world was experiencing the real sensation of being lost in the wilderness on a big scale, but I had been there before in smaller ways. I guess when you work in full-time music ministry you can start to confuse God's design for your life with your own work. You can start to find your own ways to measure God's plan. You can start to measure life with your own maps: Is the crowd big enough? Is my song number one on the radio? Am I speaking to enough people about God? How many people came down to the altar call last night?

But when everything is quiet and stripped away, when you can no longer do the things under your own power that you assume are part of God's plan, you learn something even truer about our God: He is more interested in you than in what you do for Him. I had already experienced a time in my life when I couldn't play the guitar because of a serious hand injury. And I had lived through a season of silence where I lost my voice and couldn't speak or sing for close to two months. Times like these felt like direct threats to what I thought made me important to God and to the world. I had been in places where my direction apps quit working and I wondered, *God, what is the plan?* And ironically those were the very moments when I felt God closest to me. Those were the times when He was working to bring me back to Him. Those were the blue couch kind of moments that God used to remind me that no matter where I went, my home was with Him.

You know, there are few things quite as fun as being out on the road with my band, worshiping God and playing music for people. I couldn't have dreamed of a better life. Even better than playing baseball. But no matter how profound those moments are, my favorite times are always when that bus rolls back into my hometown of Nashville. My favorite moments are when I get back to my own front door, and I get to hug my girls again. The best part of navigation is always coming home.

Maybe through all the worry and anxiety in today's world about what God wants us to do, we should start with the truth that He stays with us through every twist and turn. He's with us on every back road and He is there when we think our GPS apps are failing us. Maybe when we talk about God's plan for our lives, we aren't talking about a playbook that is written out with strategies or some map that we have to follow turn by turn. And maybe the reason we are designed so uniquely is that *we* are God's plan. And if God always stays with the plan, then we can know that just like He stayed with Joseph, He will stay with us. Maybe each of us has one specific and unique part to play in His work to redeem the whole world. And what if that part is simply to embrace God's love? Maybe the greatest part of God's plan for your life is to make sure that no matter where your story takes you, in the end, you know that He loves you. I think God has no more important plan than to make sure you get back home to Him.

[CHAPTER 4]

God Stays with Imperfect People

Rebels, Prodigals, and Misfit Heroes

I was in the middle of doing one of my many online performances of 2020 when a comment from one of my listeners grabbed my attention. My heart broke as I read the question, "Is God done with me?" and watched it move quickly up my phone screen and slowly vanish into the sea of hearts, waves, fist bumps, and prayer and praise emojis. That sentence cut through everything else that was going on in my studio, and I could feel the despair in it. *Lord, please be with this person*, I prayed as I continued to sing and smile for the camera. I'll never know exactly what that person was going through in the moment to make them pose that question, but honestly, I can't tell you how many times in my life that I have asked that very same thing. In fact, just that morning, moments before I began singing, I was wrestling with how God could use someone as imperfect as me.

That morning I thought about those walks with my family and how God had come to walk with Adam and Eve in the story of Genesis. I reminded myself that God wants to walk with me. God actually *likes* me. He has designed me uniquely and has a plan for me. And I sang those song lyrics I wrote about the God who actually runs in my direction—and still I was amazed at how frequently I just don't feel worthy. So many times, I feel like I am moving in the other direction from God. It made me remember the rest of that scripture about God walking in the cool of the day. He was coming toward Adam and Eve, and the Bible says, "Then the man and his wife heard the sound of the Lord God as he was walking in the garden in the cool of the day, and they hid from the Lord God among the trees of the garden" (Gen. 3:8).

They went and hid from God out of guilt and shame for what they had done. They didn't feel worthy to walk with Him. Doesn't that capture how we feel some days? You can almost hear Adam and Eve as they hid, both thinking that same thing as the listener I was praying for: *Is God done with me?* It seems like since the beginning we have been messing up, falling short, and missing the mark. And just like Adam and Eve, we all sometimes feel like we aren't quite good enough. But why do we all wrestle with that voice?

This belief that we are not worthy of God's love is a common and destructive way of thinking. It is the voice of an enemy who comes to steal and destroy by separating us from a God who wants to be with us. To keep us hiding from the God who is pursuing us with His unique design for our lives. I have noticed that voice attacking me in three distinct ways.

First, it tells me I am not good enough, not up to the task. I am not a good enough musician and singer, not a good enough dad or husband.

It also comes to me in the form of guilt and shame. Maybe it does for you too. That idea that you are just too sinful, that God isn't going to get over that one. This voice tells me that my pride is out of control. That I just can't stop messing up. Which is all part of the lie that God's forgiveness is not complete.

And worst of all are the whispers that we are too broken for God to fix. We've messed up too many times. God can't use us because of our brokenness.

I do find some comfort talking and praying with my peers and bandmates, my accountability partners and friends, and they remind me that these are the things that they deal with too. The struggle is real!

It has been so many years since that blue couch. So many ups and downs. I know that God is always moving in my direction, but I've often wondered if I have kept Him at arm's length because of my own guilt and shame. How could I show up for God if I spent my time believing I didn't measure up? Could I help someone asking, "Is God done with me?" when there were moments that I wrestled with the same question? If He made me with a plan and a purpose, why did I feel so guilt-ridden and unworthy of His love? How could God use someone like me? I kept thinking about those three lies that the world uses to separate us from God: You aren't quite good enough. God won't be able to get over that one. God can't use someone as broken as you are. We simply can't allow ourselves to be defined by those words.

The "Not Quites" and the "Never-Get-It-Rights"

This made me think back to the beginning of my music career. When I first moved to Nashville, I assumed I would get signed to a deal right away. I figured that if I just knocked on the record label door they would open it, shake my hand, have me sign some papers, and *bam*, I'd be the next Johnny Cash! Instead, I faced flat-out rejection for three years straight. Every single record label I auditioned for turned me down. And it was always, "Don't call us, we'll call you." Occasionally, because I wanted to learn and improve my auditions, I would make the mistake of asking the record executives what they didn't like about me. The list was always longer than I expected. I let the rejection from these critics crush me: "You're not quite good enough, not quite talented enough, not quite charismatic enough, and not quite handsome enough . . ." I always laughed when they would add "quite" to the "not," like that was supposed to make me feel better! I joke sometimes now that I had many nights lying in my bed and crying out to God, "Lord, I know that last one is *not* true! I know you have blessed me with these Matthew McConaughey looks for a reason, and I will *not* hide this face under a bushel!" (That one usually gets a pretty good laugh in front of a live audience.) But man, the rejection was real. And too often, I allowed those words to define me instead of recognizing God's voice in my life.

My good friend Mark Hall from Casting Crowns and I wrote a song about dealing with rejection and the voices that tell you you're just not quite enough to measure up. We talked about how much this mindset can get in the way of embracing God's love. I remember as we wrote it, I was joking about always being the last kid picked for the kickball team and how I was always made fun of as a kid because of my weight. Mark opened up about having undiagnosed dyslexia and how it made him feel stupid and unworthy. The world can make you feel inadequate. We wrote and released a song that spoke right to the heart of the lie that we don't belong and to the truth that God sees things differently than we do. Like it says in Ephesians 2:10, "we are God's handiwork, created in Christ Jesus to do good works, which God prepared in advance for us to do." We are created to do good works! Still, it can be so hard to remember that God has a different view of us than the world does. Is it possible I am listening to the wrong voices for encouragement?

You would think that growing up in the church as a pastor's kid would have helped prepare me for a career in Christian music. You get to see some unsuspecting people act in really mean ways. And when I was young there was always the expectation to behave and talk and look a certain way because I was the preacher's son. Sometimes I didn't live up to that. But I have to be honest about the grace thing. I didn't realize until I was older that I wasn't offering those folks I saw at church a lot of grace. And in the same way I didn't offer a lot of grace to myself.

Church: Where You Have It All Together?

It is still difficult to go to church sometimes because I feel like I am always on stage, and I don't want to let people down by looking at my phone or nodding off during a sermon. When you are a public Christian, musician, pastor, or evangelist, it feels like you have to put on a little bit of a Christian "Hulk Hogan" persona because you know that people have expectations of how you should look and act.

It kind of reminds me of when I was seconds away from doing a live television interview. I was led by the stage manager to two matching chairs where I was seated next to the host of the show. She was holding a copy of my new book at the time. A book that had a giant close-up picture of my face on the cover. "You remind me so much of my brother," she said. "Why's that?" I asked. "Because he has a lazy eye just like you!" Nothing against having a lazy eye, but I actually don't have one. And even if I did, well, not cool, lady! Not cool! To make matters worse, the very next thing I heard was the director shouting, "And we are live in 5 . . . 4 . . . 3 . . . 2 . . . 1!" I spent the entire interview wondering if what she said was somehow true and I just hadn't noticed for forty years. A nervous sweat began to invade my forehead as my eye began nervously twitching, a natural reaction from the shock of the amateur diagnosis I had just received. As patient as I attempt to be with people, I felt a lot of pressure to keep my cool. Later, I realized how much we strive for and want perfection in everything we do. I felt the pressure to be perfectly polite in that situation, even though it was tough.

Sometimes in church we talk about grace and love, but what we really expect is perfection. We talk about the fact that we all have fallen short, and we all are sinful, but we dress up and pretend that we are blameless. Sometimes I wish church started a little bit more like a recovery meeting where we just admitted our faults right out of the gate: "Hi, I'm Matthew West, and I'm a sinner and have fallen short of the glory of God." And the congregation would say, "Hey, Matthew." Maybe we are looking in all the wrong places for approval. No one is perfect, and yet sometimes it feels like we expect perfect appearances inside the walls of the church. As a result, I meet so many people who believe God won't stay with them because of their imperfections, when the exact opposite is true. God always chose the imperfect people to do His best work. In fact, if you look through the Bible, you will notice that He seems to go for those second-stringers, the not-quites, the people who don't seem to have it all together. He chooses them for His team. He uses them to do His most important stuff.

It is interesting to pay close attention to the Bible characters we think of as the great heroes. Why? Because they were all completely flawed. They were the people who had the biggest mess-ups. They were the ones who lied, cheated, ran away, or worse. Let's just start with Abraham in the Old Testament, who was so cowardly he even lied about his own wife, claiming she was his sister so the king wouldn't kill him. There was Moses, the guy who led Israel out of slavery, who actually murdered an Egyptian soldier and then ran away to hide from the authorities. He also begged God not to send him to see Pharoah and tried to come up with excuse after excuse for why he wasn't qualified for the job. Then, of course, the prophet Jonah ran away from God's calling so fast that it took a giant fish to convince him to do anything right. And King David, who was the author of many of the psalms and the man the Bible calls "a man after [God's] own heart (1 Sam. 13:14)," had an affair with a woman named Bathsheba—and didn't just stop there. He murdered her husband, who also happened to be one of his top generals, in order to hide the fact that David had gotten her pregnant. The prophet Elijah, the very guy who watched God bring down fire from the sky in front of a bunch of angry Baal worshipers, hid in a cave when things weren't going his way. And that is just a handful of people from the Old Testament.

Carefully read through the genealogy of Jesus in the book of Matthew, and you will find that the people included in Jesus' family tree are some questionable characters: liars, adulterers, murderers, even a prostitute. But what about the twelve men who were closest to Jesus? The guys called to be His disciples were all outcasts in one way or another. One might have even had a lazy eye! Many of them were fishermen who weren't smart or wealthy enough to make the cut and stay in school past their fifteenth birthday. One of them was a tax collector who was detested by his own people. The disciples were the dropouts and the second-string players of their day.

My favorite of all of them is Peter. His name means "the rock." Peter was one of the biggest talkers in the group of disciples. He swore he would stand by Jesus through thick and thin. But he was the very one who denied he even knew Jesus three different times. Despite this monumental mess-up, Peter was the disciple whom Jesus later chose to build His church: "And I tell you that you are Peter, and on this rock I will build my church, and the gates of Hades will not overcome it" (Matt. 16:18). It's pretty clear throughout the Bible that God not only hangs out with the imperfect people but He seems to choose them to do His most important work! If God can use these people, maybe we should be a little bolder and more confident that Jesus can use us as well.

Are You Ever Too Broken for God?

God uses us in all our imperfections because of His grace. He seems to fortify the areas where we are weak just to show us His strength. I am constantly in awe of God's grace toward me. I think that is why I write about it so much. I remember being invited to a writing retreat at a place that used to be owned by the iconic country singer Alan Jackson. He had recently sold it, and the new owners wanted to have some Jesus songs written in the same space where so many famous country songs were written. I remember driving out to that cabin in Franklin, Tennessee, and it was like a cowboy's palace. It was a stunning property fit for a king (think cattle on a thousand hills).

The main house looked more like the residence of a Hollywood star or DC dignitary, with big white columns and enough square footage to house every artist on Nashville's Music Row and their family members. As a songwriter, I felt a little intimidated coming to work at a place like this. The road that led to where I would be working was long and winding and led all the way to the back of the property, where a modest two-bedroom log cabin rested in the woods on the edge of the river. I remember walking up to that cabin with the big palace behind me over my shoulder and thinking, *This is about right. I don't belong in the mansion.* Yet even stepping into the simpler log cabin humbled me. This was where so many famous songs had been written, and I felt like I didn't belong. But God took that sentiment and turned it into lines about His grace. That cabin is where I wrote the first words to the song "Broken Things," about being a beggar in the presence of a King.

You know what's most interesting about the new owner of the Southern mansion and the property where that little cabin rested? Alan Jackson sold it to a guy who made his fortune thanks to some creative ingenuity. He is a self-described junkyard dog. An expert on everything about cars and car parts. His business takes cars that have been totaled in a wreck and finds a way to salvage and sell the seemingly worthless car parts for a profit. A hefty profit. An "I could buy Alan Jackson's megamansion" kind of profit. When you look through the pages of the Bible, you learn that God is in the junkyard business too. If we pay attention, we'll notice He is always working beautiful results out of the broken things in our lives. He takes what others may see as worthless and says, "I see value. I see purpose. I see a way to redeem this." I am so glad that God doesn't avoid the junkyards of our lives. Even more, He willingly steps into them and says, "For by grace you have been saved . . ." (Ephesians 2:8).

God of the Junkyard

For several days after my virtual show, I kept thinking about those words I'd seen scroll across my phone: "Is God done with me?" And I kept hearing the voice of my cab driver singing my own song back to me: "The One who runs in my direction when the whole world walks away . . ." Grace is what I sing about so often because it is what I've always needed. It makes me think of those verses in Ephesians 2: "For it is by grace you have been saved, through faith—and this is not from yourselves, it is the gift of God—not by works, so that no one can boast" (vv. 8–9).

One of my favorite things about traveling the country with my job is how I get to see all the amazing stories of the work God is doing in the lives of ordinary people. It seems like God takes the very things that break us and uses them to heal others. He is always working through our weakness to make us the best versions of ourselves. There are too many incredible stories to tell you and too many amazing people to recount. But I can remember two that stand out as proof that God uses us in our brokenness.

I met my friend Rusty from the Quad Cities of Iowa and Illinois several years ago. Rusty spent years making one mistake after another, always in trouble with the law, and in and out of jail. Now he is the executive director of a ministry called One Eighty. He met Jesus while he was serving time behind bars. And that is when God gave him the dream to start an organization to help people like him. Rusty told me that a few years after getting out of prison, he launched his ministry with the help of some friends and $500 to buy a trailer. God took Rusty's brokenness and turned it into his strength. God took a man in prison who was willing and faithful and used him to grow a ministry that now works to bring hope, love, and opportunity to people and communities dealing with crises, poverty, and addiction. And the One Eighty ministry is bold about the fact that they help people build a relationship with Jesus.

In Florida, I had the privilege to meet Eric Smallridge and Renee Napier. They have an incredible story of grace and redemption. In 2002, Eric was driving drunk and killed Renee's daughter, Meagan, and Meagan's friend Lisa in a horrible car accident. He was sentenced to twenty-two years in prison. Renee came to forgive Eric even while grieving the loss of her daughter, and in turn Eric decided to make something positive out of his tragic mistake. Less than two years after Meagan's death, Renee began giving DUI presentations to high schools, colleges, military groups, churches, and DUI offenders. Since 2004, she has reached over a hundred thousand people with her talk about Eric's decision to drink and drive and the healing power of forgiveness. Eric was granted permission to join Renee in her speaking campaign back in 2010. He captures the audience by boldly recounting the crash and his life in prison. Renee and Eric end every presentation with a compelling embrace.

It's amazing to see a mother embracing the man who was responsible for her daughter's unnecessary death. I've witnessed it with my own eyes inside the walls of a maximum-security Florida prison, singing and leading worship for an audience of inmates who were all serving life sentences. With Renee on my left and Eric on my right, we lifted the words of the song "Forgiveness" and watched hands go up and tears fall down as a crowd in orange prison uniforms praised the God who is in the junkyard business. It is humbling to see how God is using their relationship to educate and heal other people. It is an incredible reminder of the way God works in the world. We are never too broken or too imperfect for God to stay with us. And it is never too late for God to use us. Maybe that has been my problem all along. Maybe I tend to forget who truly defines my worth and my identity.

The Disgrace of Downers Grove

Just a few miles from where the six-time NBA Champions competed night after night, another group of champions played—the Downers Grove junior varsity boys basketball team. And on that team was a young Matthew West. Yes, I owned a pair of Air Jordans, but that was where all of the athletic comparisons between me and the famous #23 who played for our Chicago

Bulls ended. I was one of five guys who didn't play all the time, but when we did, the coach would substitute us all in at the same time. He told us to play as hard as we could for a few minutes and not to worry if we committed a foul on the other team. We may have occupied the bench and been the second team in practice, but we had created our own identity. We were called the "mad dogs." We would run hard, dive on the floor, and be tough while the starters were on the bench catching their breath. I like to think we were the "muscle" of the team. Now, we couldn't hit a shot to save our lives, but we would wear out the other team while we were in the game. Our coach was a tough guy, and he would humiliate us at times if we didn't do the right thing. There were some long, hard, miserable practices where I remember him telling me I might be better off on a different team as he pointed to the cheerleading squad practicing their pyramid at the other end of the gym. Ouch.

But this story isn't really about basketball. It is a lesson about grace and who we allow to define us. Of course, everyone knew I was the preacher's kid, and there were certain expectations for behavior that came along with that. And most of the time, I lived up to those as best I could. But one time, our team was playing a particularly close game against one of our rival high schools, and we came to that moment in the contest when the coach looked at the bench and yelled for the mad dogs. Into the game I went. A few minutes later, I remember getting called for a foul and having an un-preacher's-kid-like word leave my lips at one of those rare quiet moments in the gym.

It felt like it was happening in slow motion. The word was

coming out like one of those bubbles in a cartoon and I wanted to reach out and grab it and put it back and eat it before anyone could hear. But it was too late. The referees gave me a technical foul and I was ejected from the game! The coach was furious with my foul and my vulgar response, and he began to scream so loud that the entire gym could hear him: "Matthew West, *you* are a disgrace to this team, the school, and the entire town of Downers Grove!" I walked back to the locker room humiliated. I knew my dad was in the crowd. I knew everyone had heard me and the coach. I was embarrassed and felt so much shame.

I wanted to tell you this story because, yes, I messed up and in that moment in front of the whole gym, that coach named me "a disgrace." What I've learned is that the world will do that to you from time to time. Sometimes you'll be the hero; sometimes you'll be the disgrace. I don't remember anything about the result of that basketball game. I can't even remember the final score. And I certainly don't remember anything the coach said to me after the game. But I do remember that as I came out of the locker room, my dad just put his arm around my shoulders as we walked to the car and said, "Love you, son."

You know, there are ups and downs in life. You can't pay too much attention to the praise or the criticism. You can't be tempted to find your identity in either one. It hit me later that Dad was just reminding me of who I truly was in that moment: I was his, and he loved me. Dad still grounded me for the bad word I said, but thinking back on that moment makes me see how God has been there for me the same way when I've messed up. If I'll just keep my eyes on Him, He'll walk with His arm around me and remind me who I am—His son.

That understanding might explain why if you google "Matthew West lyrics," you'll see the word *grace* everywhere you look. It is at the heart of everything I write because I know how badly I need God's grace. I have to sing it all the time to remind myself it is like oxygen to my soul. I wrote a song on my last record called "The Man Who Needed Grace." The lyrics are pretty straightforward: "Once upon a time, there was a man who needed grace, with a trail of bad decisions left behind him . . . feeling like forgiveness could never find him." That is me so often. I need grace in the ways I take control over my own life. I need grace for the ways that my spiritual life can sometimes feel like an obligation. I need grace for my moodiness. Grace for my rough edges. Grace for the dark corners of my character. Grace for the times when I give in to temptation. Grace for me, and grace for other people. I need grace for the ways I am always telling myself I don't measure up.

We all face those lies that we aren't good enough, we can't be forgiven, or we are just too broken for God to use us. I smile as I think of how God has taken the "Disgrace of Downers Grove" and inspired me to write a whole bunch of songs and even a few books about my favorite word in the English language: *grace*. I wonder if you've ever felt the heavy weight those three extra letters, D-I-S, can heap onto your weary soul. What have you been told you're the "disgrace of"? Have you ever felt like the disgrace of your family? The disgrace of your church? The disgrace of your profession? The disgrace of the whole school? Or maybe your junkyard is one that only you know about and the question that flashed across my cell phone—"Is God done with me?"—circles around in your mind like a broken record spinning the same song over and over again.

Disgrace is a heavy word. But remember that God wasn't done with Peter, the "disgrace of the disciples." He wasn't done with Jonah, the "disgrace in the belly of a fish." He wasn't done with David, the "disgrace of his kingdom." And He's not done with you. You've heard the old cliché, "One man's trash is another man's treasure." What if you dared to believe that one sinner's junkyard is our Savior's treasure? Throughout history God has been lifting up and removing those three heavy letters, D-I-S, one soul at time. I think He is running straight for you with arms open wide.

[CHAPTER 5]

God Stays Out of Safe Spaces

Singing Jesus Songs in Biker Bars

In a season when every television program, every news app, every social media post seemed to be focused on how we should barricade ourselves in to stay safe and keep others safe, even simple things we took for granted—like eating at a crowded restaurant or hugging a friend—suddenly presented risk. But from the security of the Story House studio in my backyard, I was able to reach out into the world with a new virtual weekly devotional time and with my online performances. It was a weekly reminder of the thousands of prayer requests, needs, and hurting people in the world. It was a constant reality check that life doesn't offer us any promises of safety.

The prayer requests that came in each week from people experiencing illness, job loss, grief, and anxiety sent me poring over the Bible for encouraging stories and verses to share. I needed hope. I think we all needed encouragement during those long days of isolation and bad news. And as I studied God's Word, I realized that out of all the promises in the Bible—of all the love and grace and hope God offered me—being safe wasn't ever one of them. In fact, following Jesus seemed to be the opposite of a safe life.

I thought again of Adam and Eve walking with God and the moment that they left the safety of the garden and stepped into the wider world. I wondered how scared they must've felt. Did they question whether God would continue to walk with them? I was reminded of a line I found from a Christian author named Frederick Buechner, who wrote, "Here is the world. Beautiful and terrible things will happen. Don't be afraid."[1] It seemed the whole world was afraid. I read about the disciples, the men and women who followed the same Jesus I had met on that blue couch as a teenager, and how they lived exciting, exhilarating, and even dangerous lives. These men and women were "canceled" by the Pharisees and the leaders of their religious culture, they were thrown in jail, they were often beaten or stoned, and many of them were eventually killed—for following Jesus! None of these people in the New Testament seemed to be obsessed with "playing it safe," but they were also right in the middle of all the exciting action that God was doing in the world. They were performing miracles. They had a front-row seat to witness signs and wonders. They were seeing God move in extraordinary ways precisely because they were unwilling to stay where it was safe.

I noticed that in the Bible Jesus was constantly calling people into action with commands like "go" and "follow Me." As I thought back over my life and the times that I felt closest to God, I realized they were the moments when I was going and doing and focused on His work, following the passions that He had given me, working to share His love. When I focused my time and energy on His command to love my neighbor, it was always green lights. Jesus never issued safety instructions or stay-in-place orders. When we spend all our time working to protect and preserve ourselves, maybe we are missing out on God's will for us. I laughed about the idea of having to wear a hazmat suit to play music for people some-day. But it made me think: What if when we are so concerned with keeping dangers of the world out, we end up missing out on the chance to enter into the good that God is doing?

What if when you get consumed with being safe, you can't see the work that God is doing in the unsafe world? What if finding the kind of life that Jesus calls "life to the fullest" has nothing to do with playing it safe? "Shelter in place" was a reminder that safety is an illusion, but it was also a call to (eventually) get back out into the world and experience the life God has for us. Maybe I needed to strip down out of my spiritual hazmat suit! Maybe I wasn't meant to rest on the comfortable blue couch of my life. And maybe that blue couch experience was my catalyst and my constant reminder to go out into the world and to fol-low Him.

God's Deliverance in a Clapton Song

You would think that singing is a pretty "safe" job, right? What's the worst that can happen—a sore throat? A callus on my fingers from playing too much guitar? When I was in college and just starting out in music, my rule was simple: never turn down an opportunity to play in front of people. I wanted to get better, so I would perform anywhere. Birthday parties, school assemblies, backyard barbeques, church potlucks, bar mitzvahs, weddings, funerals, fraternities, sororities, youth group meetings, homes for the elderly, karaoke contests, living rooms, street corners, and smoke-filled bars—if someone would let me play my guitar and sing, my answer was yes. And that is how I ended up taking a gig at a local biker bar opening for a band that had achieved "regional acclaim" called Russian Roulette.

The band's name tells you all you need to know. But allow me to give you a bit more detail. Let's just say this rock band was much like the shopping mall in the town where I went to college: stuck in the '80s—tight pants, eyeliner, and enough Aqua Net hairspray in their hair to set that dive bar on fire if someone got too close with a cigarette. The promoter's promise to pay me forty bucks for the gig blinded me from the very real possibility that the crowd at this bar might not exactly be my desired demographic. But when you're a college student, forty bucks is a small fortune.

I brought my college friend Joey along with me that day, and it took one step inside that bar to realize we were no longer inside the safety of our little college campus. This was a rough-around-the-edges place for rough-around-the-edges folks. One of our first major observations when we walked in the door was that everyone in the place was drinking out of plastic cups. We were curious and asked the manager about it. He explained with a shrug, "We don't want people to have glass bottles when a fight breaks out." I took notice that the manager didn't bother to use the word *if*; he clearly said "when" a fight breaks out. Apparently, a fight breaking out was a foregone conclusion. Forget pre-show butterflies. I was a nervous wreck. But I set up on the stage of the smoky bar with a small dance floor and prepared to play my set. I looked out into a sea of tables filled with people who were decked out in tattoos, leather jackets, leather boots, leather faces, and suspicious looks. So much leather.

Here goes nothing, I thought, as I began to play my first song. There I was, acoustic coffeehouse college kid, playing my own songs about "God and girls" in front of the roughest audience I had ever seen. It only took two songs for me to realize that no one was paying attention, and those who were listening were getting cranky. At that point in my career, I knew how to play only a handful of songs outside of the ones I had written. But the situation was getting desperate. Just ten minutes into my performance I started into a silent prayer that I doubt anyone has ever prayed before or since: *Jesus, please help me play a Bon Jovi song!* I was desperate to remember any rock song I had ever heard before. *Lord, do You know the words to "Jack and Diane"?* I prayed, hoping maybe they were John Mellencamp fans. By the grace of God, I was able to string together an acoustic rock set that I have not performed since. For my final song, I began to strum the chords to the famous Eric Clapton song "Wonderful Tonight." I just couldn't remember all the words.

I had heard of preachers asking the Lord to give them the words to say in a sermon before, but this kind of prayer took on a whole different meaning. Just like Jon Bon Jovi, I was "livin' on a prayer." The crowd was beginning to grumble and stare and point at me. I started to play the Clapton song while continuing my earnest prayer that the good Lord would somehow help me remember the second verse. Immediately, the floor in front of me crowded with couples who began to slow dance to the song. And miraculously, as I continued to play, the words of each verse kept coming to me in the way I imagined manna fell from heaven for the Israelites in the wilderness.

In the meantime, on that dance floor right in front of me, there were couples making moves in ways that this preacher's kid could never have imagined anyone slow dancing. Let's just say, these leather-clad couples were so close they didn't leave any room for the Holy Spirit! I can testify that no Matthew West performance before or since ever caused such a questionable scene. As I finished my song to cheers from the lovebirds on the dance floor, my friend Joey finally caught my attention from the back of the room with his frantic hand gestures. I rambled something into the microphone about taking a quick break and snuck off the stage to see why Joey was so alarmed. The music began to blare from the bar as I stepped away from the microphone, and new clouds of smoke drifted across the room.

Joey leaned in so I could hear him and said, "We have to get out of here *right now*, Matthew." He explained that he had just overheard some guys who were doing drugs in the bathroom say they were going to grab my guitar and beat me with it! Remembering those strange looks I was getting from the edges of the crowd, I didn't second-guess Joey's assessment. I grabbed my guitar and with our heads down we made for the parking lot as fast as we could. We drove away from that biker bar relieved that we had escaped with our lives and with my guitar intact.

Of all my early performances, that night still stands out to me. Would I have gone to play at that bar if I had known what was going to happen? Nope. And I never did get my forty bucks payout for playing that night either. All these years later, I'm still waiting for that one person to come up to me after a concert and say, "The first time I ever saw you play is when you opened for Russian Roulette!" But I honestly wouldn't trade that moment for anything because I grew in that experience.

I learned that if I could get up and play music in front of that kind of hostility, I could play anywhere. I learned how prayer can save my life! But I also learned that if I trusted God, He would give me the words I needed right on time. Maybe God was just prepping me for the times that I'd get to go perform at correctional facilities. Who knows? Maybe someday I'll get Russian Roulette to open for a Matthew West concert. Seriously though, when I think about that adventure, I realize how I would've been robbed of growth (and a really great story) if I would've chosen to play it safe. It turns out that stepping out of our safe places can teach us to trust God!

Pick Up Your Cross and Follow

Jesus' command for exactly how we are supposed to become disciples gets uncomfortably specific. He said that we should pick up our own cross and follow Him. It doesn't sound like He was asking us to hide away in places where we are safe from harm. But what does that mean for us? In Acts 16:22–24, I read about how the apostles went out to share the good news about Jesus with people, and do you know what happened to them? "The crowd joined in the attack against Paul and Silas, and the magistrates ordered them to be stripped and beaten with rods. After they had been severely flogged, they were thrown into prison, and the jailer was commanded to guard them carefully. When he received these orders, he put them in the inner cell and fastened their feet in the stocks." That's what they got for telling people about the love of Jesus? Throughout the Bible we see example after example of how the people who followed God and made the biggest difference in the world were always the ones who refused to play it safe!

Just think about some of the Bible characters we have talked about already. It wasn't exactly the safe choice for Moses to go to Pharoah and demand that he free the Israelites from slavery. Joseph wasn't really playing it safe when he spoke up to share his dream interpretations from prison. Joshua didn't choose the safest war strategy by marching around Jericho with trumpets. Gideon certainly didn't embrace a safe plan of action when he followed God's directions to prepare for war by cutting his army from thirty-two thousand men down to only three hundred.

David could've stayed in the pastures with the sheep instead of grabbing a rock and taking it to a sword fight against a giant named Goliath. Of course, the disciples didn't make safe choices by leaving their fishing business and their families behind to follow Jesus. Jesus Himself invited five thousand people to stay for dinner one evening with only five loaves of bread and two fish. Paul didn't play it safe by insisting on going to Rome to preach the gospel.

All of these great stories in the Bible have one thing in common. At the center of each one is a person willing to step out of their safe space, take a risk, make a leap—and maybe that kind of trust is the secret formula to participating in God's remarkable miracles. When God's people get beyond their own safety and security, seas get parted, giants fall, city walls crumble, armies are defeated, a boy's lunch feeds five thousand, lepers are healed, the dead are raised, the blind see, and sinners find salvation. All these works are miraculous, but they are never safe!

That Time a YouTube Post Got Me Canceled

Trying to live the "life to the fullest" that Jesus desires for us can also put us in the line of fire. Many of you reading this book may know that I did a video with my daughters for a song called "Modest Is Hottest." Google it and you'll find some interesting takes. If you know me at all, you'll know how I like to try to bring some laughter and joy to the world. Some of my favorite artists are comedians, and I always love when I can bring levity to people's lives as a songwriter. So, in the middle of some hard times, I wrote some funny songs. One in particular made my daughters laugh. To be honest, I also wrote it because I get tired of some of the ways pop culture pushes crazy stuff on our kids. I quickly recorded a video for the song and shared it on YouTube. I had recently produced another song during the pandemic called "Quarantine Life" that helped people find laughter during a difficult time. This newest song was meant to make people smile; it was a tune written from the perspective of an overprotective dad of teenage daughters. I didn't see anything offensive about it. I filmed it with my daughters, and we laughed and had a great time. They wore turtlenecks in the summer as we sang the lyrics "what the boys really love is a turtleneck and a sensible pair of slacks. Honey, modest is hottest, sincerely, your dad." Everyone in the Matthew West camp got the humor in it. But I was about to learn a valuable lesson about where I put my focus and whose approval I should be seeking with my life.

Let's just say that when the cancel culture crowd comes after you, you quickly realize that no one in your life is off-limits or safe. People quickly began to write their own narratives into my song. I was being attacked with words and phrases and philosophies I had never even heard of before. In just a few short days, I had to make the decision to take down the video because people were beginning to attack my teenage daughters. The whole thing was stunning. It was an eye-opening moment because I love to try to reach people with humor. I enjoy introducing the love of God to folks while they are laughing.

But the attacks about this song came from all sides—the left and the right, Christians and non-Christians. I had people mad at me for what they perceived I was saying in the video and people upset at me for "caving to cancel culture" and taking the video down. The statement I released about the song was not enough of an apology for some and too much for many. It was a difficult few weeks, but just like all my other experiences, I was thankful for what it taught me about God. It reminded me that maybe I had been looking for approval in the wrong places. It helped me remember that I live for an audience of One. God doesn't care about the likes and blue check marks. The only thing He cancels is my past mistakes so that I can be free to follow Him. And if I am faithful to the gifts God has given me, His approval is all I need.

World Changers Don't Stay in Their Safe Space

God continues to show me that the life He wants for me is just beyond my comfort zone. Each time I move out of the places that feel safe, He seems to bring new life. It has forced me to think bigger and do some things that scared me. I had always dreamed about doing new forms of media to connect with my audience and people in ministry, music, and entertainment who I admire. But I never really knew what that would look like until the quarantine grounded me at home for almost a year.

During that time, what seemed to be the thing that could end my career in the music business turned into a period of real growth. I wrote songs every day, began writing this book, and also launched *The Matthew West Podcast*. The podcast was a stretch that ended up being a new creative outlet that I really fell in love with. I was excited about the chance to learn how to become a good interviewer. But the best surprise of this new adventure was that I was able to spend time with friends who were living life to the fullest and doing inspiring work in the world. It gave me a new opportunity to talk to people who had made the choice to run away from a safe life. Their incredible stories were a weekly inspiration of what it truly looks like to follow Jesus.

I was able to talk with my friend Bethany Hamilton, a surfer who is still chasing after the big wave. There was a film made in 2011 called *Soul Surfer* that was based on her life. At the age of thirteen, as a rising surf star, Bethany was out surfing when she lost her left arm to a fourteen-foot tiger shark, which seemed to end her career. Most people would've quit surfing after something like that. I think most of us would have never gone in the ocean again. The water would've become a dangerous place. But just one month after the attack, Bethany was out surfing again, and within two years she had won her first national surfing title! She now encourages others to face their own adversities by sharing her journey. She talks about God's grace and His plan for her life. She tells people, "With Him I am unstoppable."[2] Her story is incredible. At seventeen years old, just three years after the accident, she realized her dream of surfing professionally and is still an active surf competitor to this day. She is living life to the fullest and inspiring people in her wake.

The podcast also allowed me to connect with my friend

Christine Caine and hear her story about the time she was standing in an airport in South Africa and saw a picture of a missing girl, and how God used that moment to show her the horrors of human trafficking. She had a safe life as a successful Christian writer and leader at Hillsong Church. But she heard God's call and knew that she couldn't stay in place. She had to do something. Since 2008, she and her husband, Nick, have been fighting against human trafficking in all its ugly forms all over the world through the A21 Campaign. She heard Jesus' call to go, and she did.

I also had the opportunity to have Sam Acho on my podcast to talk about the ways he is working to impact communities all over the world. Sam is a retired professional football player and sports analyst for ESPN. He believes the world needs less religion and more relationships. He loves Jesus. He had the money and a successful career, and he had accomplished all he ever wanted to accomplish, but he knew God was calling him to do more. Sam joins his parents and siblings to work with Living Hope Christian Ministries' medical missions and serve rural communities in Nigeria. With the help of his family, Sam has also spearheaded a campaign to raise money for the building of much-needed hospital in Nigeria. As a former University of Texas Academic All-American, Sam stresses the importance of reading and education as he visits schools, signing autographs and speaking with kids.

Sam had some great stories to tell about God moving in the world when we willingly get out of our safe spaces. He talked about the time he took the owner of the Chicago Bears to visit prisons. He also shared the story of the time he had to sit out practice and games because of an injury. Rather than feeling sorry for himself, he had gathered some other professional athletes and worked to rehab an old liquor store and turn it into a desperately needed grocery store in a Chicago neighborhood that didn't have access to healthy food. When you listen to Sam talk, it is obvious how many lives God has changed because of his willingness to leave comfort behind.

These are just some of the many amazing people who are witnesses to what God will do with your life if you leave the safety of your own little space. I am amazed every week by the stories of how God takes our willingness and turns it into works of wonder. I leave each podcast interview inspired that the miracles we read about in the Bible still happen every day through the hands and feet of people who are simply willing to take that first step and follow Jesus. With every inspiring story, I feel the question rising up in my heart, "Are you willing?"

Parachutes, Prayers, and No What-Ifs

Once the initial pandemic lockdowns were over, I had some pent-up adventure energy from those months of being holed up in one place. The funny thing about our safe spaces is that the same things you use to shut yourself in from the scary things in the world are also the things that can shut out the beautiful things about the world. Maybe it was my Enneagram number, or maybe I simply had so much enthusiasm to get out and do the things I couldn't do when the pandemic was raging, but I launched into a summer of no "what-ifs" by taking a pretty big risk. It was an idea that started with a few lines I had written down for a song called "What If" about what it looked like to live life to the fullest. I had been thinking about how God wanted me to live the rest of my life: To go. To follow. But I was also about to learn that the first step is always the scariest.

You'll never guess where the "What If" song experience led me! The plane had taken off late in the day when all the professional skydivers were going out for their own jumps after work. I was sitting right there at the edge of an airplane doorway with my feet dangling thousands of feet up in the air. I was the only rookie diver on the plane that evening. "The pilot is taking us higher so that we get to have a longer free fall," the other divers explained. As I looked out with all of Middle Tennessee spread out underneath my toes like a patchwork quilt, I knew there was no way to back out. I had an entire film crew with me to capture footage of my first plane jump for the "What If" music video. The skydiver assigned to me was wearing a pink helmet with a bright mohawk on it. Just as I was being positioned at the door of the plane, he jokingly shouted, "You'll be fine. And if your parachute doesn't open, don't bother screaming because it will be too late anyway!" *Not funny, blue mohawk guy. Not. Funny. At. All.*

Let me pause here to tell you the truth about being pushed out of an airplane. While it may be a great metaphor for getting out of our safe spaces and this may be a fun story to read, it is absolutely terrifying. I was never going to be ready to jump, but we did it anyway. I was attached to the pink helmet skydiver and things happened in that one-minute free fall that will impact me for eternity. The other skydivers flew around me during our dive, spinning me in the air in circles. I was finding it hard to think and a little difficult to breathe. And I don't know how many times a man can recommit his life to Jesus in one minute, but I may have set the record as I spun and fell. A whole bunch of blue couch moments! Who needs an altar call when you can just jump out of an airplane?

The dive took just a few frantic minutes, and the first sixty seconds was the scariest part, free-falling with the earth racing toward me and prayers on my lips. Finally, the pink helmet guy pulled the cord of our parachute. It jerked me up in the air and let me experience a very brief three seconds of calm and peace as I was just high enough to appreciate the beauty of the area where we would safely land. I could probably write a chapter in my next book about parachutes and God's grace.

Everyone I talked to as we were boarding the plane that day said that once I experienced my first skydive, I would be hooked on the adrenaline and become a lifelong skydiving enthusiast like them. They said I would want to do it again and again . . . which was completely false. It was not true at all. This grown man fell from the sky and then fell to his knees, kissed the ground, and praised Jesus as loudly as he could as soon as he landed safely. He also swore to never jump out of an airplane again.

I had volunteered to skydive for that music video because I wanted to push myself and I saw it as the perfect metaphor to challenge other people to step out into the unknown spaces of their own lives. I wanted to challenge myself to be bold. But that experience reminded me that every new day is like a trust fall into the arms of God. Each new opportunity that we step into is like skydiving with the Creator of the universe in charge of our parachute. Can we choose to stay in that plane and play it safe? Yes. But we will also miss out on the excitement, the joy, and the exhilaration of the jump. When we move away from the safety, we get to see God move in the world.

This Isn't a Self-Improvement Plan

As I sat in the Story House and dreamed about all the things I would do when the world opened up again, it also made me look back on my life and consider the things I had not yet done. Where were the places God was calling me that I had been too scared to go? I knew that the story of God is the story of the One who stays with us. He walks with me and talks with me. I thought of the good news and how Jesus was always commanding us to move: to follow, to go forth. Why? I don't think Jesus was talking about a self-improvement plan. But He knew what life to the fullest could look like.

Maybe He wants us out there beyond our safe spaces to live into His commands for us: "Love one another. As I have loved you, so you must love one another. By this everyone will know that you are my disciples, if you love one another" (John 13:34–35). Everything I see happening in our world is stirring within me a greater desire to be bold in my faith, not timid. But at the same time, I can't help but feel that Jesus is telling us that the boldest act of faith we can deliver to this hurting world is the bold act of love. Will I leave my safe spaces in response to Jesus, even if it costs me everything? May we jump out of the plane in such a way that people will say, "Look at the way they love their fellow man!"

Whenever I get tempted to look at all the scary and unsafe things happening in the world and ask, "God, what are You doing?" maybe I need to pay closer attention to the people who are working in the middle of the mess. The people who love Jesus seem to be the ones who run toward those situations. It is the doctors and nurses in the ICU during a pandemic. It is the people who get out of their safe spaces and run to the rescue. It is the Sam Achos working in inner-city Chicago and Nigeria. It's the Bethany Hamiltons surfing the next big wave and challenging Christians to make a difference in the world. It's the Christine Caines fighting the darkness of human trafficking on a global scale. It is you and me when we decide that God is calling us to more than just a safe life. That is when we see God show up and do miraculous things. It is when we look in the mirror and decide we aren't going to live our lives with any what-ifs. When we understand that we are living for an audience of One, when we move beyond our safe spaces—that is when life to the fullest begins. That is where the miracles happen!

CHAPTER 6

God Stays with Those in Need

Eyes Up and Flashlights Out

Early on during quarantine, I decided to start doing a consistent devotional time online. Being a songwriter, I decided I had to come up with a clever title, so I called it "Quarantine Quiet Time." (I'll give you a second here to really soak it in and appreciate my use of alliteration.) My hope was to reach out and connect with people through that strange season of isolation. The plan was to go live on social media until the world got back to normal and this "little virus thing" we were dealing with blew over. I am still doing these live devotions weekly (but the word "quarantine" just got too depressing, so now we simply refer to it as Quiet Time, or QT). This practice has allowed me to stay connected to the needs beyond my neighborhood and provided our community a chance to pray for one another. Each week we read about the heartbreaks, fears, failures, grief, depression, illnesses . . . and the list goes on: "Pray for me; I'm lonely." Or, "Pray for my mom; she is in the nursing home and has COVID."

"Pray for me, pray for me, pray for me . . ." The messages continue to come in by the thousands. It is my constant reminder that our world needs hope and prayer and action. And the more I allow Jesus to invade my heart, the more He turns my attention toward the needs of a hurting world. Every prayer request is a reminder that my calling that began in a blue couch moment goes far beyond music.

What Are Your Greatest Hits?

In the quiet moments of the past year, as I took time to consider how God walks with me, how He leads me, His grace for me, and how He pushes me out of my safe spaces, I've been acutely aware of how my legacy as a child of God has *nothing* to do with how many acclaimed three-minute songs I've written. My worth as a person isn't connected to Grammy nominations or Dove Awards or greatest hits or the number of people who have sung my songs back to me at a show. I felt like I "arrived" as a song-writer when the record company called and said they wanted to do a greatest hits album. (Of course, it could've meant that they were sick of me and were just trying to fulfill one more record on my deal to get through my contract!) But in reality, music is a tough business, and I have been fortunate to have the privilege of people listening to my music long enough to actually have a greatest hits compilation.

I'll admit, when I first started out in this business as a young musician, I thought being famous was a big deal. I craved the applause of the crowd. I used to obsess over whether I was going to get that Monday morning phone call from my record label telling me I had a number one song. But God has shown me in so many miraculous ways that the best recording I could ever make, the best tracks I could ever lay down, aren't ever in the studio. What will go down in history as my true "greatest hits" are the ways that I loved other people.

The more I've tuned in to God's love, the more I've wanted to tune my life outward toward others. The more I surrender my life to God, the more I have found Him pushing my attention toward the needs beyond my usual focus: me. He wants me to use the light He has brought to my life as a beacon of hope and a flashlight to look for the ways I can love my neighbor. He wants me to lift my eyes up and notice the needs around me. I'm always moved by the advice of Mother Teresa when she won the Nobel Peace Prize: if you want to change the world, first go and love the people closest to you, your family and your neighbors.[1] I've wondered what kind of witness I would be if I went out and sang songs about knowing the love of God but didn't even know my own kids. What good would it be if I got to the end of my life having built a successful career but I never did anything for my neighbors? I don't want that to be my legacy.

A Matthew 25 Way of Life

Several years ago, I felt God pushing me to refocus my ministry. It began with the simple vision I had of turning the microphone around and pointing it back to my audience. I hit a place in my work where I didn't feel fulfilled by just singing *at* people; I wanted to do life *with* people, and I felt God was calling me in that direction. But what began with the simple step to take people's stories and turn them into songs, God quickly took and grew into a nonprofit ministry called popwe, which evolved into something much more beautiful than I had ever planned it to be. You see, as we carved out this space for folks to share their stories, something unexpected happened. We began to see how God's light was shining through those broken places in their lives and transforming the world. What started as a creative experiment quickly transformed into an active and thriving nonprofit organization.

We launched the popwe ministry with three guiding principles. First, every single human being is crafted in the image of God to do good works in the world. Second, God's power is expressed through our own weaknesses and vulnerability. If we will boldly share the stories of what God is doing in our lives, it will shine the light of hope into the lives of others. And finally, we hoped to challenge one another to live out the love of Jesus in the world. It quickly became an opportunity for people to connect and get involved as a community to help others. God began using popwe as a hub to empower my community to step in and do work that was more important than any greatest hits record. And as popwe grew into what it is today, it helped me see how God was calling us into a life of prayer, and to address the needs of our neighbors and offer our presence to them—just as He offers His presence to us, and to address the needs of our neighbors. Popwe helped remind me that if God ever produced a greatest hits record, you and I and our neighbors would all be on it. (Okay . . . and angels . . . there would probably be some angels singing too.)

The Bible is clear that our blue couch moments should be the catalysts to get involved in one another's stories. Jesus calls us to love and to care for those in need. He preached in the Beatitudes that it is the poor, the hungry, and the grieving who will be blessed. In Matthew 25, He got straight to the point:

> "For I was hungry and you gave me something to eat, I was thirsty and you gave me something to drink, I was a stranger and you invited me in, I needed clothes and you clothed me, I was sick and you looked after me, I was in prison and you came to visit me."
>
> Then the righteous will answer him, "Lord, when did we see you hungry and feed you, or thirsty and give you something to drink? When did we see you a stranger and invite you in, or needing clothes and clothe you? When did we see you sick or in prison and go to visit you?"

> The King will reply, "Truly I tell you, whatever you did
> for one of the least of these brothers and sisters of mine, you
> did for me." (vv. 35–40)

That is some hard-hitting stuff in the New Testament. Jesus didn't mess around. He got right to what is required of us when we embrace His kingdom. He made it crystal clear what it means to follow Him; He was saying that our blue couch experiences should be our stimulus for a Matthew 25 way of life. To know Jesus is to live with your eyes up and flashlights out looking for the chance to help your neighbors.

Get Out of Your Comfort Zone, but Don't Eat the Goat

Popwe partners with so many great ministries already doing incredible work around the world. My desire is to use every platform I get, whether it be a concert stage, podcast episode, or even this book, to point others to Matthew 25 opportunities like Compassion International. Compassion is a leading authority in holistic child development through sponsorship. We really love to connect people to them, and I encourage you, if you aren't already, to get involved and sponsor one of their children at compassion.com. Compassion is the only child sponsorship program validated through independent research, and that means they do what they promise they will do. They work through almost seven thousand churches to help children in twenty-six countries and have rescued over 1.9 million babies, children, and young adults from poverty. They do some great work in Haiti, and I took the band there on a life-changing trip and was even able to visit with a child whom I sponsor.

Now before I get to the details of this story, you should know that there is a certain skill set one develops as a preacher's kid. Growing up with parents in the ministry, you are *always* being invited to a potluck or over to someone's home for lunch after church services. That means when I was a kid in Illinois, I ate some great meals—but I was also served some interesting dishes that forced me to learn how to push food around my plate and be loquacious enough to avoid having to actually eat anything that wasn't particularly appetizing.

My band arrived in Haiti, and we spent the day shooting video footage for Compassion International using a new song I had written called "Do Something." There is a line in the song about how easy it is to "live like angels of apathy" when it comes to serving and taking care of the needs of others. As we were shooting the video and writing prop signs, we noticed that the video producer had misspelled that very important line as "*angles* of apathy." We all laughed and gave him a hard time. But it still worked. Too often it is our own *angles*—our personal points of view and our limited ideas about the world—that can lead to apathy and keep us from engaging. Nothing opens our eyes to the needs of the world like getting involved with an organization like Compassion.

The greatest blessing of that trip was to go visit one of my sponsored children. We spent an incredible day with our gracious hosts in a small village outside of Port-au-Prince. And my training as a pastor's kid really came in handy when dinner began. I'm out on tour a lot, so I know what's on the menu at Cracker Barrel, Chick-fil-A, and Wendy's—but throw me a strange fish with spiky skin still attached to it, and I promise I won't know what to do with it except to let my preacher's kid instincts kick in. I started talking while feverishly using my fork and knife to cut my food and push it around my plate so no one would notice that not a single bite actually ever touched my lips.

Directly behind our table was a field where I noticed a few goats and some chickens just minding their own business. But looking at the menu, I quickly realized their looming fate. In addition to my spiky fish, guess what was being served? Goat and chicken. When you are dining in these types of situations, especially in small villages, the whole farm-to-table thing gets real! I noticed my drummer, Dustin, ordered the goat. Maybe it was because of the way the goat had given me the side-eye from the field before we sat down to eat, but this was just one of those instances when we all had the same bad feeling about something. The same one we all get while inspecting food under the gas station heat lamps at a 2:00 a.m. tour bus stop. All of us, that is, except for Dustin. As inconspicuously as I could, I leaned over and tried to let him know that he shouldn't eat the goat. In fact, I think the entire band was trying to find low-key ways to get his attention and say, "Don't eat the goat." But my man wasn't just eating the goat; he was going to town on that plate of goat meat. In fact, he may have had several helpings. In the end, we all had a great time at dinner with our company and forgot all about the goat . . . until the next day.

The following morning as we were being driven to the airport, the goat came back to everyone's attention. We found Dustin doubled over in pain. The poor guy had gotten so sick from food poisoning that he was near the point of hospitalization. We decided that we just needed to get him home. I'm sure he will never forget that flight! The best part is that ever since that trip, Dustin's fantasy football team name has been "Don't Eat the Goat." As awful as that meal was for Dustin, it is a great story and a funny reminder of the joy we experienced on the ground visiting in Haiti. Our work with Compassion changed our lives and expanded our hearts.

I think we can easily become desensitized by the frequency of crisis after crisis on our phone screens, news feeds, and flat-screen televisions. We don't intend to, but it can quickly turn us into "angels of apathy." And apathy is dangerous thing. When we can sit in our living rooms and simply consume the hurts of the world from the safe distance of a screen, it somehow insulates us from the real pain and the deep needs that our brothers and sisters are facing. I can become numb without noticing, indifferent to the suffering around me. But everything that Jesus calls us to do as we follow Him is the opposite of apathy. I'm reminded again of John 15:12–13, where Jesus said, "My command is this: Love each other as I have loved you. Greater love has no one than this: to lay down one's life for one's friends." Wow. There isn't any nuance in what Jesus is saying there. We are called to love others in a *sacrificial* way.

Whenever I can get out of my own safe space, my worries and my routines, I can be awake to the needs of others.

The entire band left Haiti feeling that way. Of course, we had a healthy respect for eating goat, but more important, we had a new love for the people of Haiti and the issues they face. Haiti was no longer a story on a screen. The experience of meeting the little boy, Geralson, whom my family and I sponsor, was a moment that instantly jarred me from any apathetic slumber. He isn't just some long-distance recipient of a monthly check that my family sent or the occasional letter my daughters would write. He is real. He is human. He is beautiful and precious. He needed help. He was hungry and I had the chance to give him something to eat. He was thirsty and Compassion International made sure he had something to drink. This reminds me of another story about Haiti that taught me how God can use our everyday faithfulness to reach the world.

Start in Your Own Backyard

I love Eugene Peterson's translation of Matthew 10:5–8 in *The Message* where Jesus said, "Don't begin by traveling to some far-off place to convert unbelievers. And don't try to be dramatic by tackling some public enemy. Go to the lost, confused people right here in the neighborhood. Tell them that the kingdom is here. Bring health to the sick. Raise the dead. Touch the untouchables. Kick out the demons. You have been treated generously, so live generously." Wow. We've been treated generously, so live generously. I can't help but notice there is no hint of apathy anywhere in this command. But the thing I love about these verses is how they point to the truth that loving the world can begin in your own neighborhood.

I have friends in Cincinnati who have a powerful story of impacting Haiti, and they have never stepped foot on the island. Instead, they skipped a Saturday of sports and took their four children to work at their church packing food supplies that would be shipped to Haiti. The church cleared out the sanctuary, brought in the supplies—along with music, lunch, and plenty of laughter—and spent an entire day working to fill a tractor trailer full of food that wouldn't spoil. Churches all over the Midwest spent that weekend doing the same thing. It was an incredible accomplishment. All those trailers of food were loaded onto a cargo ship that sailed for Haiti. However, weeks later, my friends heard the sad news that the ship full of food was stopped in the harbor of the capital city and left to sit. It seemed all that work those churches did to help feed the hungry of Haiti was for nothing. But God had a different plan.

That boat was stuck in the harbor at Port-au-Prince for over a year because of regulations and red tape from the Haitian government. But then the 2008 hurricanes struck and much of the island was devastated. The food shortage in the aftermath was overwhelming. Just as the city of Port-au-Prince and surrounding villages were in dire need, that ship full of food floating in the harbor was unloaded and distributed as part of the rescue efforts in the aftermath of an unforeseen natural disaster. What looked like a failed plan was actually God's perfect timing. And all those church communities that showed up together to spend the day volunteering to help their neighbors in another country had the opportunity to witness God using their faithfulness to rescue people a year later at the most critical time.

Be a Witness to the "Withness" of God

God has taught me not only the importance of serving but also the power of simply sitting with people in need. I don't think you have to travel the world to experience this, but I've learned that when you come close to the needs of the world, you also find yourself close to Jesus. That sentence works in reverse order, too, doesn't it? The closer you are to Jesus, the closer you'll find yourself to the needs of the world He's calling you to pay attention to.

I once traveled to a town in El Salvador that was the birthplace of one of the world's most dangerous gangs. I was there to visit another Compassion International village. As we drove into the town that day, we literally drove past a dead body lying on the side of the road. It was unnerving. It was very clear we weren't in a safe area.

We were visiting a Compassion village not far from the capital city. There was a river nearby and the tide was very low, and it caused a stench in the surrounding neighborhood that was really something. I remember stepping into the village and feeling as if the work Compassion was doing there introduced a bright light shining through in the middle of the violence, poverty, and darkness all around us. I was introduced to another little boy whom my family sponsors and was told that he was very shy. Not knowing how else to communicate with him, I knelt down to his level, made eye contact, and smiled.

It's hard to explain, but I experienced a moment where I became aware of the full scene: the violence outside in the streets, the smell from the trash and the river, the extreme heat, the orphans all around me, and the people who had dedicated their lives to serving Jesus in that place—and somehow it was one of the most beautiful experiences of my life. I didn't want to be anywhere else in the world. The kingdom of God, the very presence of God in that place, was tangible in a way I have witnessed only a few times. Immanuel was in every square foot of that room. I wasn't thinking about my tour, my next song, my kids' college plans, the bills, the hundreds of details it takes to run a ministry—all of that was trivial. I was witness to the presence of God with those little orphans. I was fully awake to what God was doing in the world. The blue couch wasn't in my childhood home in Downers Grove; it was right there in El Salvador. Billy Graham's voice was replaced by the laughter, tears, and chatter of those little Spanish voices playing games. I was experiencing one of the catalyst moments that would reorient my faith forever. In that moment, I was a witness to the "withness" of the God who stays. And that moment continues to inspire me to keep doing something each day to change the world for the better.

The Challenge to Just Do Something

I could write a whole book just about the people I've had the chance to meet through popwe who are busy making God's greatest hits. You need to know about Jordan. He was a two-sport all-star athlete in high school and went on to run track and play football at a university in Kentucky. During his sophomore season, he broke his ankle, and that is when he received his first prescription for oxycodone. His story is not uncommon. Addiction to these pain meds quickly caused his life to spin out of control. After two failed drug tests, the university kicked him out and revoked his sports scholarships. Jordan needed help, and his parents stepped in and convinced him to go to Teen Challenge in North Carolina. If you aren't familiar with the organization, they offer time and space for broken people and those recovering from addiction to experience God's grace. Jordan explains that it was during his time in Teen Challenge that he began to realize that God was just getting started with him. He talks about how God gave him a new story and freed him from being an addict the rest of his life. Since his recovery, Jordan has gone back and earned his master's degree from the very college that kicked him out. Now he is a teacher, a coach, a husband, and a father. Jordan now shares his story to help inspire young people and is using his light to lead people toward recovery. He is doing God's work right there in his own neighborhood. Maybe getting involved in Teen Challenge is your Matthew 25 calling.

My friend Andrea is the inspiration for the song I told you about called "Do Something." She is a former University of Colorado student who spent a semester abroad learning about microfinancing in Uganda. While there, she visited an orphanage that was in critical condition. The children were being badly neglected and abused. She was heartbroken for the orphans who had no advocate, and she decided she had to do something. She refused to leave the children and return to the United States until something was done to improve the conditions of the orphanage.

By sheer determination and her refusal to give up, Andrea and her sister convinced the Ugandan government to close that orphanage, which left about eighty children with no place to go. You know what happened next? The government handed the children over to her—a foreign college student! Andrea brought this need back to the States with a new vision and desire to create a safe place for these children to grow and learn. That was the catalyst for the creation of Musana (which means "sunshine"). It is now a thriving orphanage in Iganga, Uganda, housing over one hundred children. Andrea prefers to spend most of her time in Uganda, reaching the world and bringing hope to people one helpless child at a time. The thing that was so moving about her story was that when she was asked what it was that made her fight for those children in Uganda, she simply said, "I just kept thinking, if I don't do something, who will?" She didn't rationalize and overthink it; she didn't listen to all the voices that told her it was impossible—rather, she went to the extreme to show us what wild abandon to the cause of Christ looks like. I would challenge you to pray about joining Andrea and getting involved with the Musana Community Development Organization.

I think stories like Andrea's and Jordan's should inspire us all to use our God-given talents to serve those in need wherever we can. When we witness God working in the lives of those who are simply willing to say yes to His calling and His transformation, it can help us focus our vision in the right place. Both of them faced different challenges, but they turned them into opportunities to help others. And these young people are a testament to the fact that faith is action. They have their eyes up and their flashlights out. They have taught me that following God isn't about the talking. It's about doing.

A Different Kind of ROI

I can still get so overwhelmed about how much need there is in the world. I don't know about you, but it can make me feel a little helpless and distant. I often get busy managing my own little space and focusing on tours and bills and recording sessions, and I forget what it looks like to truly make a difference. What God teaches me over and over is that His command to love one another isn't super complicated. In *The Message* version of Matthew 10, the chapter ends with Jesus challenging His listeners: "This is a large work I've called you into, but don't be overwhelmed by it. It's best to start small. Give a cool cup of water to someone who is thirsty, for instance" (vv. 41–42). It can be as simple as when my wife, Emily, arranges a dinner to be delivered to a family in need. When I make time to go and pray with a friend. It can be like my Cincinnati friends skipping a Saturday at the ball field to go to church and make food packets for Haiti. Or it can be simply sitting in the presence of the people who need you. You don't have to travel to Haiti or Africa or El Salvador to do God's work. Caring for people in need usually starts with small, faithful acts of love. That is when the "with-ness" of God gets real. Those are blue couch experiences; they are truly the greatest hits.

And that is just the thing about the blue couch moments when you experience God's love. Those moments foster a beautiful responsibility. They reorient your life so that you don't get so wrapped up in the business side of life that you forget the kingdom business. James 2:15–17 says, "Suppose a brother or a sister is without clothes and daily food. If one of you says to them, 'Go in peace; keep warm and well fed,' but does nothing about their physical needs, what good is it? In the same way, faith by itself, if it is not accompanied by action, is dead." Unless we are willing to do the work, to love one another, our faith is dead and useless. What I am learning is that the blue couch is more than an experience; it is a calling. God's love and grace that He gives freely through that blue couch experience brings with it a beautiful cost. You see, the kingdom of God has a much different take on ROI (return on investment) than we do. That beautiful cost to you is a sacrifice that will transform you from the inside out and help you focus on life's eternal greatest hits.

To Be a Champion of Others

If our life's greatest hits will be our Matthew 25 moments, then my friend Cindy had enough in her lifetime for a double album. Cindy was a real champion. Not the Muhammad Ali kind, and not the "first one crossing the finish line while cameras flash" kind either. Cindy was a champion *of* others. She was a champion of mine. She worked every day on Music Row in Nashville in the world of music publishing. She was passionate about the power of a song and discovering songwriters with potential who just needed someone to open the door for them. That's what she did for me. Cindy was the first industry professional who ever gave my songs a listen.

Her passion and excitement for the music I was writing led her to make sure that everyone, and I mean *everyone*, on Music Row knew my name and heard my songs. She was the first to celebrate with me when an artist recorded one of my songs and the first to encourage me on the many occasions when I faced rejection from record labels. She believed in me—the kind of belief that even made *me* believe in me. And I can't ever write a single song without thinking about how Cindy made me believe I could do it.

Cindy was diagnosed with an aggressive form of cancer and passed away at a very young fifty years of age. Among those in attendance to say goodbye were one songwriter after another whom she had championed. But it wasn't just the music industry that came to say thank you to their champion. What many people didn't know about Cindy was that being a supporter and champion of others was not just part of her professional life. It was how she lived her *whole* life. She had a standing appointment every single Sunday night at a women's prison in Tennessee. She helped lead worship and ministered faithfully to these women behind bars week after week, month after month, year after year.

I knew not to call her on Sunday nights. That's how important that ministry was to her. Those women mattered to her, and she would often tell me stories about what God was doing in their lives. I even went with her once and led worship. It took one visit for me to see why this ministry mattered to Cindy and also to see what Cindy meant to those women.

I sang Cindy's favorite worship song at the memorial service and tried to fight back tears. I'll never forget when the pallbearers came forward to carry Cindy's casket. They were all formerly incarcerated women from the very prison where Cindy faithfully ministered. They had come to say goodbye to their champion as well. She believed in them when nobody else did, and they knew their lives were forever changed because of her. Cindy had her eyes up. She had her flashlight out. She thought less of herself, more of God, and much of others. She made everyone around her know they mattered. From the big-time music industry executives to the incarcerated criminal, the ones in the limelight and the least of these. Could people say the same about me? What if I've spent so much time trying to write my greatest hits that I've forgotten the most meaningful melody of all? What if it's not too late to get to work on a different kind of legacy, a double album of greatest hits that has nothing to do with me and everything to do with those Matthew 25 moments—feed the hungry, clothe the naked, and serve like Jesus?

CHAPTER 7

God Stays in Times of Anxiety and Fear

Cool, Calm, Collected, and Other Stuff I Don't Have in Common with Tom Brady

I think we can all say we've experienced a season when all the right unpredictable ingredients created the kind of metaphorical waves that could sink our metaphorical ships. Perhaps you've seen the George Clooney movie *The Perfect Storm*, which was based on historical events. There was an actual "perfect storm" in October of 1991 off the New England coast. The storm took place over Halloween. They called it a "perfect" storm because of all the meteorological factors that had to line up just perfectly for it to happen. I've read it was the merging of a hurricane from the tropics and a strong storm system coming out of Canada with just the right weather patterns at just the right time to create hundred-foot waves and winds up to eighty-five miles per hour.[1] It also made for a pretty intense movie about the Massachusetts fishermen who died tragically on their boat, the *Andrea Gail*, during that storm.

Into the Perfect Storm

The images of the huge, powerful waves crashing over the helpless fishing boat on the big silver screen have always stuck with me. The overwhelming force of that storm evokes the same emotions and feelings of helplessness that I've experienced recently. Each roar of our "Roaring Twenties" seems like it is the next giant wave of bad news getting ready to crash into us. If you google "pandemic" or any new catchphrase related to the choose-your-own-world-crisis book of the early 2020s, you'll find article after article about how it is all taking a toll on our mental health and emotional well-being. Studies show that more people feel more alone and more afraid than ever before. If you are even in earshot of the news cycle, it can send you into a state of anxiousness and panic. I know anxiety and fear aren't unique to our lifetimes, but they sure do seem more prevalent than ever.

I don't have all the answers about how to handle this unpredictable world, but I do hope to be a calm and steady presence in the world for my family, my friends, and my neighbors.

I don't want to live wrapped up in anxiety or fear about how my world is unfolding. I wish I could wake up every day and go about my life the way Tom Brady plays on the football field. I read recently that he may be the most celebrated athlete in the history of American sports. I mean, have you ever seen that guy play? I've watched him in the biggest games on the biggest stages against the toughest teams, and it never seems to matter the score or how much time is left on the clock; he always appears to be cool, calm, and collected. I know it's only football, but sometimes I wonder what allows the Tom Bradys of the world to be able to maintain that kind of calm under pressure.

Seriously though, even if you're one of the lucky few whose past couple of years have been smooth sailing, we've all faced chaos at some point in our lives. And many of us have experienced the kind of perfect storms where we couldn't feel God's presence or see how He was working.

There have been some moments in the past year where I felt that way as I watched the news and read the prayer requests filling up my comments during Quiet Time. I've definitely faced some moments when anxiety and fear have gotten the best of me. The unfolding chaos of the world has made me examine how and where God "stays" during those times.

Keeping Our Boats from Sinking

Is God really with me when I feel alone or anxious or afraid? I know that same question has been at the front of everyone's mind in this new age of pandemics and social and political unrest. In this "perfect storm," there are also subtle changes to everyday life that I've noticed affecting me. We carry around devices that provide the blessing and the curse of instant connection and instant feedback. We can receive all the bad news in the world instantaneously. We also have social media applications so that we can be reminded that our vacation isn't as cool as our neighbor's vacation. We can spend our days comparing our lives to the social media stars who shoot with just the right lighting, just the right filters, and just the right angles in an effort to influence us. So, even when the roaring of our news cycle seems calm for a moment, our lives are noisier and more chaotic and unsettling than ever.

It makes sense that people feel more alone and scared right now. Anxiety and fear are pervasive and real, and I think it is important to be honest about the fact that we all deal with it. I've read that, in the United States alone, over forty million adults over the age of eighteen deal with anxiety.[2] And I recently saw a statistic from 2020 that one out of four young adults (ages eighteen to twenty-four) admitted to having at least one suicidal thought in the past year.[3] That is heartbreaking for me to think about. One of my daughter's classmates, Sam, was one of the sweetest kids I've met. But nobody knew that even at a young age he was fighting a very real battle with depression. The first week of seventh grade, Sam took his own life. His family and the entire student body were absolutely rocked by the reality that such tragedy could hit so close to home and that depression could steal the life of a young man who should have had his whole life ahead of him.

I watched a special that comedian Gary Gulman did called *The Great Depresh*. He talks candidly about how debilitating his ongoing battle with depression is at times. In one bit, he explains that he went through a whole season where the only thing he could get out of bed to do was watch an episode of the television show *Better Call Saul*. These are difficult times; I see the effects of anxiety and depression everywhere these days—and followers of Jesus are not immune to it. When we as Christians talk about those challenges in terms of being a "lack of faith" thing, I think we get it wrong. There are times when we need professional help. We need doctors and medicine and treatments and interventions—the tools God has given us. We need to get rid of the stigma related to talking about our mental health. We need to be more open and honest about those truths. We are all just trying to keep our boats from sinking in the middle of a perfect storm.

Panic at the Disco (Um, the MRI Room)

Some days when I look at the world, I have to remind myself of one of my favorite verses, Joshua 1:9: "Be strong and courageous. Do not be afraid; do not be discouraged, for the LORD your God will be with you wherever you go." I know from experience that you can tell yourself that truth repeatedly and still experience anxiety, which feels anything but strong and courageous. In those moments, it seems impossible to feel cool, calm, and collected. Anxiety is common these days. So is depression, and it does not discriminate. I have friends and family who have battled with anxiety, but I never really understood what they were talking about . . . until I did. Until it hit me out of the blue in the form of a panic attack.

Being on a tour across the country and seeing America through a bus window is every musician's dream. It's still cool when we get to stop at good restaurants and meet great people from town to town. I still enjoy everything about bus life with one big exception—the sleeping part. I've never been able to sleep well at night as the bus rolls down the road. My band members tell me they sleep like babies, while I toss and turn. My story about anxiety begins with sleeping on the tour bus a few years ago. I woke up one morning with terrible pain in my neck. Maybe the bus had hit a pothole? Maybe the driver had slammed on the brakes and threw me around as I slept? Who knows? Whatever I did that night, my neck hurt for weeks before I finally went to a doctor about it. The doctor immediately scheduled an MRI to make sure there wasn't anything significantly wrong. I had never had an MRI before. I thought it all sounded easy enough.

I arrived at the appointment and went into an observation room with the nurse, where she showed me the giant machine they used for the test. The nurse asked, "Are you claustrophobic?" I laughed just to prove my manliness, and thought, *I'm not a child.* I told her confidently, "No, I am not claustrophobic." She responded with reassurance, "Good, then it will be easy for you." As I assessed the setup through the observation window, I convinced myself that I may even be able to nap during the test. No sweat. The nurse instructed me that I would need to stay completely still. I went into the room and laid down on the bed with the pillow under my knees, and then the noise started. The machine turned on and pulled me into a round tube where I could hear the nurse talk to me through a speaker on the inside. I closed my eyes and settled in for a few relaxing moments. No sweat, right?

But something happened to me suddenly during the test that I had never experienced before. They had placed something around my shoulders to keep me still, and just a minute or two into the whole ordeal, a newly terrifying thought occurred to me: *You can't move!* I couldn't quite catch my breath. I started sweating profusely from head to toe. (I get a little anxious just writing about the experience now!) I was suddenly focused on the fact that I was trapped and began to squirm a little. A voice broke through from the speaker in my little tube: "Sir, you *have* to be still!" I remember yelling back at the voice, "I *am* being still!" But the next thing I knew, I was shouting as loud as I could, *"Stop! Let me out!"* I'm a little unclear on some of the details, but I may have threatened to break their very expensive equipment if they didn't set me free. I couldn't breathe and I couldn't calm myself down until the machine stopped and I was finally released from that plastic prison.

The technician stopped the test, pushed a button, and brought me out, and I was completely drenched in my own perspiration. My breathing slowed, and as I began to calm down, I felt a wave of humiliation wash over me. I kept apologizing to the nurse. Of course, if you have done an MRI before, you know that the worst part of the experience for me was that the test wasn't finished. If I wanted to find out what was wrong with my neck, I had to go back into that machine for five more minutes. Fortunately, the medical staff helped me get through it. I didn't realize until later that I had experienced my first panic attack. It was irrational and overwhelming. And in the aftermath of that test, I also realized that my reaction didn't have as much to do with the MRI as it did everything else that was going on in my life at the time. As terrible as it was, that experience has really helped me understand, connect with, and have compassion for the people in my life who face that kind of anxiety.

Maybe It's Okay That Twelve Guys Freaked Out in a Boat with Jesus

The uninvited perfect storms of modern life remind me of a sudden and furious storm in one of my favorite Bible stories found in Matthew. "Then he [Jesus] got into the boat and his disciples followed him. Suddenly a furious storm came up on the lake, so that the waves swept over the boat. But Jesus was sleeping. The disciples went and woke him, saying, 'Lord, save us! We're going to drown!' He replied, 'You of little faith, why are you so afraid?' Then he got up and rebuked the winds and the waves, and it was completely calm" (8:23–26). The Gospel of Mark tells us a little more about the fear and anxiety of the disciples in this situation: "Jesus was in the stern, sleeping on a cushion. The disciples woke him and said to him, 'Teacher, don't you care if we drown?' (4:38)." And there was Jesus, resting, unconcerned about the storm. I can't even sleep on a tour bus without hurting my neck, and Jesus was taking a nap on a boat in a storm! When I read this story, I also think about the fact that many of these twelve men with Jesus were no strangers to a boat. They were fishermen and had grown up around boats, so this probably wasn't their first rodeo with being in a storm. All three versions of the story (it is also told in Luke 8) also point out that this storm came on them suddenly out of nowhere.

Let me interject a thing or two about me and boats, because I've played on a cruise ship or two in my day. Have you ever tried to walk or steady yourself on a boat in rough waters? My oldest daughter learned how to take her first steps on a cruise ship, and we were kind of afraid that she would walk like a drunken sailor when we got her back on dry land. It can be a challenge to keep your balance on a boat. Even a big one. And playing on cruise ships is a funny thing because my prayer before every show is that we don't hit choppy waters and that people will run to the altar to find Jesus instead of running seasick to the bathroom. The fact that there is usually an all-you-can-eat buffet close by doesn't help that situation either. But as you may have already guessed, as much as I enjoy going to the beach with my kids, I'm a dry land kind of guy. I remember king salmon fishing in Alaska once when these three giant humpback whales surfaced right next to our boat. Yes, it was magnificent, but they were terrifyingly much bigger than our boat. It gave me a whole new respect for the Jonah story. I've already confessed my deep fear of sharks. So, while looking at the open water from the beach has always been restful, I prefer to keep my feet on dry land. All that to say, I can identify with those twelve guys—if I were on that boat, I would've been freaking out too.

The Bible tells us as the storm hit and the water rose, the disciples did two things. First, they freaked out: "Don't you care if we drown?" The storm must've been fierce if all of the experienced fishermen believed they could die. Then they looked to Jesus for help. The disciples had the right instinct to go to Jesus for help. They knew He was the only one who could save them in that situation. One of the things I have realized about this gospel story is that it is as much about us as it is about Jesus. I think we are all too often just like the disciples.

I've thought about this story often. I've been more aware of the different types of unexpected storms the world can bring into our lives: the grief, illness, financial loss, heartbreaks—hardships that hit us like waves breaking. And I've considered what it was really like for the twelve men who were closest to Jesus to be in that boat that was taking on water. In some ways the biggest lesson of the Bible is about trust. Whom do we trust? Do we trust that Jesus is with us in those moments? Do we trust He is ready to calm the storm?

I also thought a lot about how much I am like the disciples in my own life. Those guys walked, talked, ate, and worked with Jesus day in and day out, and still their first inclination was to panic. I think sometimes we carry around a lot of guilt when we struggle with feeling anxious, when we struggle with trust, or even when we face things like depression. I meet a lot of people who deal with shame about not being able to trust God enough in the middle of uncertainty and chaos. But think about this: if the very guys who lived with Jesus, walked and talked with Him, and watched Him do unbelievable miracles still freaked out when things looked tough, then maybe we should cut ourselves a break. Maybe the disciples in that boat story were showing us a little bit about what it means to be human. Maybe we need to give ourselves a little grace. We all freak out, but we can also cry out to Jesus for help after we do.

And that is the ever-important end of the story that brings me back to truth. Jesus is ever present and in control when we can't manage the storms. He is there even while we freak out. He waits for us to simply turn our attention to Him to find peace. In the end, Jesus calms the storm. But it isn't really about what we *do*, because all the disciples did was look to Him. Maybe all the noise and terror and distraction of the news keeps us from recognizing that Jesus is there with us. I am still learning that it is *who I look to* for the answers that makes all the difference. If we can learn to trust Him in these situations, it can bring a calm to whatever storm we face. I don't know if I've ever experienced a time when it has been more obvious that there is only one place I can put my trust. There is nothing solid or steady except for Jesus. In some ways the storm is a good reminder to all of us that we can't put our trust in our health, in our wealth, or even in our own ingenuity. The world has reminded us of that very clearly.

You, Sir, Are No Tom Brady

Just like with the disciples, it is sometimes difficult for us to recognize that Jesus is actually with us. We get fixated on all that we can't control. Anxiety and fear are always going to make us reach for something. Unfortunately, too often in my life, I've opted for distraction instead of deliverance. When my phone and my television fill up with storm clouds, you know what I choose instead of leaning on Jesus? Block Puzzle. That's right. For me, it's the mindless games on my phone. For someone else it might be several glasses of bourbon or binge-watching *The Office*, but we all choose where we look when chaos starts to dump water into our boats. Those moments when I should be leaning into Scripture or prayer or meditating on the presence of Jesus in my boat, I too often choose the easy out or the temporary distraction instead.

During the first months of the pandemic, when the whole world was crashing around us, I couldn't look away. I was so wrapped up with anxiety and fear, and I was addicted to the news. We were in the middle of that "un" season of a new reality. Every minute of the news was filled with *un*certainty, *un*precedented events, *un*employment. At this point in my life when I hear a word that begins with "un," I cover my ears. We've even got *un*identified flying objects! That's how bad it's been in our world, that the reports of UFOs don't even make long-term headline news. But rather than leaning into trust and looking to Jesus, instead of leading my family calmly, I spent my time obsessing over the news.

And then my wife, Emily, found a list that our daughter had written of all the things that were going wrong in the world. She sat me down and told me that I needed to do a better job of leading the family. She explained that everyone in the house was feeding off my anxiety and obsession with the latest bad news. She confronted me with a critical moment for our whole family. She told me that I had to get it together and lead our family toward peace and away from panic. I needed to hear every word Emily was speaking to me in that moment. She was right. I knew that I was choosing to look to the wrong places in the middle of that storm. I turned off the noise and distraction and focused on the One who was in my boat. We sat down together as a family and rewrote that list of bad events in the world with a list full of our blessings, the things we were thankful for, and where we saw God at work in those tumultuous times. The storm helped us refocus on trusting Jesus as a family.

The Real Giants of Trust

I have learned some life-changing lessons about trust from people at the center of life's scariest storms. I want to tell you about two of the spiritual giants who have touched my life in recent years. They've taught me that no matter the circumstances we face, no matter how troubled or anxious our situation, we can always put our trust in Jesus. They are life-lights in the darkness and my saints of trust; they make the Tom Bradys of the world look like JV players. There are times when I am so humbled and grateful to be in the presence of certain people and be witness to God's work in their story. There are times when I see God move so powerfully that it changes me as a person. I continue to tell their stories when I can, and I pray that God will teach me to trust like these heroes of mine.

I wrote a song for my friend Brooke called "Never Ever Give Up." She was a special young lady who endured a terrible eight-year battle with neuroblastoma. I spent some special moments with her over the years. I had the chance to go with my friend Elisabeth Hasselbeck to visit Brooke at the Children's Hospital of Philadelphia, and later Brooke was my special guest at a big music awards show called the K-LOVE Fan Awards. Brooke was full of life, even as she was fighting *for* her life. She once walked onto my tour bus to give a pep talk to my band, and you know what she told them? Not to screw up! She was small in stature, but her trust in Jesus was colossal. She lifted the spirits of the people around her even when she was in the middle of her toughest battle. She was the face of bravery. She was always more concerned for others than for herself, and she had a deep peace in the middle of the chaos. On June 12, 2017, Brooke became the prettiest angel in heaven, as her mom likes to say. To be in her presence was to be with a spiritual giant. Her spirit was powerful, and she knew who was in the boat with her.

Then there is Jack, from Toledo. Jack loved his family, his four little sisters, Captain America, and baseball. But Jack loved God the most. He had to endure round after round of chemotherapy for brain cancer, but he was always calming those around him. The fundraising nonprofit in Jack's memory is called Catching Up with Jack because Jack moved from our idea of extraordinary to God's idea of extraordinary faster than the rest of us. He did it with trust. When anyone tried to comfort Jack, he would simply tell them, "I trust Jesus." When the chaos of the storm grew big and the waves became too much, Jack knew who was in his boat. I was blessed to be able to take part in a fundraiser in Jack's name this past year and was reminded that heroes like him are the mightiest testaments to God's faithfulness.

Jack's legacy, just like Brooke's, is one of bringing courage and care to the families and children who are now walking through similar storms. Everyone who loved Brooke and Jack and was touched by their lives is heartbroken—but hopeful for the day we will get to see them again. Brooke and Jack left a legacy of indomitable faith in Jesus. These children were titans of trust. When I read scriptures where Jesus talks about the faith of children, I know what He means, because I had the privilege of coming into contact with these two. These beautiful souls are a few of the heroes of my faith journey who have shown me what it looks like to trust amid life's storms.

God has taught me that the truest kind of trust doesn't mean the absence of fear and anxiety. Sometimes trust means you move forward with your hands shaking and butterflies in your stomach as the storm rages all around you. Trust is about keeping our eyes on Jesus and taking that next step into the unknown. Trust means that you move forward with your eyes on Jesus no matter the outcome.

Trust Starts with the Fundamentals

I am still coming to terms with the fact that aside from our stunning good looks, athleticism, impeccable sense of style, beautiful wives, and graceful aging, there is very little that I have in common with Tom Brady. I'm just not that cool and calm and collected under pressure. But as I have read about the seven-time Super Bowl champion, I've learned that it is no accident when he seems to have it all together in the most pressure-packed game situations. TB12 spends a ton of time focused on the fundamentals. He has developed a deep trust and a confidence that if he does each step of his job, everything will be okay. Occasionally he doesn't win. But he always stays cool under pressure because he is committed to his practice.

It made me think about the fundamentals of my faith. The truth of the good news is that if we focus on Jesus, no matter what happens in the world around us, everything will be okay. If we keep our eyes on the One in our boat who loves us, even if our boat goes down, we will be with Him. During that time in the pandemic, I had to turn off the television each morning and practice the fundamentals of my faith. I opened my Bible to read. I spent less time talking and more time quiet in prayer. I dedicated more of my day to worship and meditating on Scripture. These practices helped me build trust in Jesus. Because no matter the storm, He is my only answer.

In the middle of these perfect storms, with the wind raging and waves crashing into us, we can simply lose sight of who is truly in charge. The reality is that we cannot control life any more than the crew of the *Andrea Gail* could control the waves in that perfect storm. I can't control what happens in the world any more than the disciples could control the storm coming out of nowhere on the Sea of Galilee. I began to laugh at how frequently "times like these" was thrown around on the news. The reality is that we will always be living in times like these. Times where I can't control how I am thought of by others. I can't control how my work is received. I can't even control when I will get sick. Even the long list of things I believe I'm in control of are mostly just an illusion! And times like these are all we have.

Understanding that God stays through times of fear and anxiety is about getting back to the fundamentals. I don't need to be like Tom Brady all the time if I know I've got Jesus in my boat. Getting back to the fundamentals reminds me of the truth from that old Sunday school song we used to sing: "He's Got the Whole World in His Hands."[4] And that is just the thing. God isn't just in the boat. He parts the water. He walks on the water too. He is bigger than the storm.

Getting back to the basics of the God who stays means that we remember He truly has the whole world in His hands. Isaiah assures us, "You will keep in perfect peace those whose minds are steadfast, because they trust in you" (26:3). I wrote a song during those early days of the pandemic called "Take Heart." I wrote it to remind myself and my family of the truth of John 16:33: "I have told you these things, so that in me you may have peace. In this world you will have trouble. But take heart! I have overcome the world!" The chorus is a prayer I've been hanging on to when storm clouds start to gather:

So take heart
Take a breath
Let Me lift that heavy weight up off your chest
Take My hand
I know it's lookin' dark
When the world falls all around you
I won't let you fall apart
Take heart

Maybe I can't always be calm, cool, and collected, but I am always free to choose *whom* I look to for help when the perfect storms of life come out of nowhere. I am learning that anxious times will always be with us, but the lesson that God wants us to learn is that He will be there with us too.

[CHAPTER 8]

God Stays for the Party

Naked Dancing and Drive-By Birthday Bashes

It is a little-known fact that when I was in college, I sometimes went by the name "Marty the One-Man Party." I've always loved laughter and joy and parties and cake. Especially cake. When I was young our church had cake for every important occasion, and it was awesome. I once threw a birthday party for my wife and I heard that Michael W. Smith's mom made the best Southern layer cakes. So, I hired Smitty's mom to make around fifteen cakes for the party. It was way more cake than we needed for the number of guests invited. But in my humble opinion, you can never have enough. My college nickname was evidence that I enjoy a good time. The irony is that I don't always feel very much like a one-man party. Especially through these past few years.

We've all experienced a season where the music went off and the lights went out and we had a collective moment of standing there awkwardly with our punch bowls empty and our hands in our pockets. This has been a time when football games were played in front of huge stadiums that were uncomfortably quiet and empty. A year when no one had a home-field advantage. Our Olympic athletes competed without the fans to cheer them on. Playing online concerts without a live audience took some getting used to. I went from the immediate feedback of fans singing along with me in front of the stage to seeing hand claps and smiley faces floating up my iPhone screen. The energy of people coming together to celebrate was absent during those early days of 2020, and for good reason. I have already mentioned how the normalcy was stripped away from us during that time and how it made us look more closely at what we did have to be thankful for. It helped me focus on gratitude and return to the truth that I serve a God who stays faithfully with us through every season of life.

"Down in My Heart, Where?"

Setting all the other stuff aside, I realized that if Jesus has set me free, if He has delivered me from my sins and given me eternal life—all things that I know to be true—then isn't that reason enough to celebrate? The enforced quiet of those wilderness days of quarantine made me lean in a little closer for the joy. It made me miss the party. It also made me wonder why we don't celebrate more often. When did Marty the One-Man Party get to be such a stick in the mud? If I believe that Jesus stays in the boat with me through life's storms, shouldn't I live with a deep sense of joy? Shouldn't I seek to find the party in each day?

The truth is, it is often so much easier for me to try to bring joy to other people than to allow myself to experience it. Turns out that Marty is only Marty when the party is for someone else! When times feel a little tough, I tend to want to lighten people up. I love when I can make people laugh. That's one reason I wrote "Quarantine Life" and put it up on YouTube in the middle of all that boredom and uncertainty. It's why I wrote the most ridiculous Thanksgiving song in the history of the world and drove parents crazy because their kids wouldn't stop singing "Gobble Gobble." (Also, it's part of the reason I wrote "Modest Is Hottest," but we've covered that already.) In that season of getting back to the fundamentals of my faith, I came across Jesus' words about joy in the New Testament and I decided to do a word search. Did you know the word *joy* is in the Bible more than 160 times? One scholar I came across noted that the word *joy* appears 88 times in the Old Testament in twenty-two books and 57 times in the New Testament in eighteen books. I think a lot of references are in Psalms, but Jesus talked about it too.

As I thought about the God who stays, who walks with me and talks with me, I thought about the deep sense of contentment

I felt in that first experience with Jesus on the blue couch of my childhood home. It wasn't just a happy feeling that comes and goes. It was fundamental to my whole person and seemed to bubble from my heart like a spring. I thought about getting baptized in my childhood church and the party that ensued after that service. You better believe there was baptism cake in the lobby after the service! Getting back to the fundamentals of my faith meant returning to the joy of following and being close to Jesus. Several times in the New Testament, Jesus said that He didn't just come to save us—He came to bring us joy: "I have told you this so that my joy may be in you and that your joy may be complete" (John 15:11). I remembered the lines from an old hymn, "Joyful, Joyful We Adore Thee."[1] And I thought of that song from summers long gone, the one that we sang at vacation Bible school: "I've got the joy, joy, joy, joy down in my heart!"[2] But the "Where?" response that you scream out when you are singing that song felt a little too real.

An Eeyore Christian

For most of us, quarantine was a time of gaining weight, shopping online, learning how to cut your own hair, and, if you are like me, learning a lot about yourself. I had been busy and actively avoiding what felt to me like this hipster Christian personal growth/personality movement called the Enneagram for several years. It was all the rage with my friends. But suddenly, I had this unexpected free time off the road, so I decided that

I would jump in and take a few tests. I'm one of those people who doesn't particularly want to be told what personality I have (is that an Enneagram wing?). I don't really like to be called a number, but I did it anyway. After testing and researching, I classified myself as a "3" on the Enneagram. Then I started listening to podcasts and reading about all the qualities of a 3, mainly to disprove that I was actually a 3, and I quickly discovered that despite not wanting to be a number . . . it was truer than true. My number 3 really got me thinking about how I can sometimes act like an Eeyore Christian. You know, the character from Winnie the Pooh who, instead of celebrating, likes to say things like, "Good morning, if it is a good morning, which I doubt" in that gloomy voice.

In all seriousness, I really felt God pushing me during this season when I had time to grow as a man of faith. Up until then, I had been doing a lot of work. Working on music, working on a podcast. Working on keeping my family and company afloat. Working on this book. It's like God was saying, "Don't let this season pass without allowing Me to work on *you*." My mind couldn't shake this thought: *It would be a shame to let this wilderness season pass me by and not be changed by it spiritually, emotionally, and relationally.* Difficult times are times of growth if we keep our eyes on God. So, after years of being scared about learning the Enneagram and dodging questions at Bible studies about my number, I embraced the learning process. I listened to podcasts, I googled articles, and I found books about the Enneagram. It was insightful to understand a little bit more about how God made me.

Now, I tell you about my number only because it relates back to our conversation about joy. You see, one of the traits of an Enneagram 3 is that I have a really hard time celebrating stuff in my own life. Other people? No problem. I love when the joy is focused elsewhere. But as soon as I finish something, there is never time to "pop the champagne"; I just find the next ladder to climb. I have a hard time waiting for the confetti to fall. I can't just allow myself to locate the joy, because I want to get to the next thing. As I considered the fundamentals of my faith, God really leaned on me about this issue. He still is. I discovered my inability to celebrate came from an irrational fear that I am never enough for my standards and never enough for God's standards. God is teaching me that I need to let the confetti fall in my life. I need to take time for gratitude and step into the joy that God brings to my life.

The Pool Dash, King David, and Spontaneous Joy

I think God wants us to celebrate what He has done in our lives because He is enough. His work is enough. Jesus' resurrection is enough. He wants us to celebrate our lives and the gifts and freedom He has given us without shame or self-consciousness. I think He wants us to approach our lives like my nephew approaches the swimming pool. Whenever Duke comes over to swim at our house, he gets so excited, it is contagious. The first time he visited, before anyone could get him changed and put his swim diaper on, he stripped down completely naked and made a break for the pool! He was so excited to go swimming that he couldn't be bothered with suiting up. He was a bundle of uninhibited joy until he jumped in and learned the reality of trying to swim without his floaties on! But here is a little-known truth about the West family: there is something genetic about that kind of response to a swimming pool. My parents tell a story about me when I was around my nephew's age. When I was four years old, we lived in an apartment building that had a pool. One day, my mom turned her back for a moment to find my proper swimming gear, and I was out the door in a flash running naked and making a beeline for the pool. By the time she caught up with me, I was near the pool. Let's just say the tenants in our building saw more cracks than the ones in the sidewalk that day. But there is something infectious about the people who get so overwhelmed with joy that they are fully in the moment.

I need the joy of those moments when I am overwhelmed with gratitude and present in what Jesus has done for me. You have to wonder why we don't always live like my nephew when he sees a swimming pool. I'm not in any way suggesting we all run around naked. Nobody needs that! But you get my point. That is the type of infectious, unadulterated joy that we should have. It is about celebrating what God has done in our lives. There are plenty of Bible stories about throwing a party to celebrate God's work, but one of my favorites is about King David because it reminds me a little bit of me and my nephew and our naked runs to the swimming pool.

The background for this biblical party is that the ark of the covenant, which represented the presence of God for the people of Israel, was found after being lost for seventy long years. It was being brought back to Jerusalem in a big parade that King David was leading. He had been working to return the ark to the capital city and had overcome one obstacle after another to get it done. The Bible says, "Wearing a linen ephod, David was dancing before the LORD with all his might, while he and all Israel were bringing up the ark of the LORD with shouts and the sound of trumpets" (2 Sam. 6:14–15). Bible scholars argue about what state of dress David was really in while he was "dancing with all his might" before the Lord. Apparently, there were people on the scene (including the king's first wife, Michal) who thought this kind of dancing and celebration was ridiculous or undignified for the king of a nation. But David didn't seem to care. His celebrating and dancing seemed full of joy without limits. There wasn't anything self-conscious or dignified about it.

It seems that David was only concerned about dancing for God and was dancing around a little underdressed for a king. Regardless, the story gives the impression that he was so carried away by God's goodness that he couldn't control himself. It reminds me of someone in the front row of a concert who is having the time of their life. Or of a four-year-old at the pool. Or a military family seeing their loved one at the airport after a year of deployment. Or the time your parents finally saw the grandkids after quarantine. This kind of joy is an act of gratitude and worship. I want to be better at it. That is the kind of zeal I want to live with and the kind of joy I want to display. We are forgiven and free, and that should bring us spontaneous joy!

When the Angels Throw a Rager

The one thing I am learning about myself and about the heart of God is that He keeps an open invitation to the kingdom, and if we are following Him, we should keep an open invitation to others as well. I believe God desires eternal joy for every one of His creations. I love how *The Message* phrases Jesus' words in Matthew 5:16: "Now that I've put you there on a hilltop, on a light stand—shine! Keep open house; be generous with your lives. By opening up to others, you'll prompt people to open up with God, this generous Father in heaven." Be generous and be open to others. It sounds like God is calling us to invite others to the party. The kingdom of God isn't the kind of party where you need a password or a secret handshake or where you have to be someone important to get an invitation.

I have a lot of stories about birthdays because we have a "go big or go home" policy about our celebrations. My love for a good birthday celebration started with my parents. When I was young, whenever I had a birthday, we didn't just invite one or two people; I always had to invite the whole grade at my school. It was very important to my parents that we didn't leave any-one out. That has carried over into my house. I feel like I live an open-house life. But sometimes I am not good at the actual hosting and inviting people over for dinner part of that. Emily is great at it. My life as a performer has me constantly surrounded by people, so my tendency isn't always to fill our house with, well, more people. But she makes sure we keep an open house. When our daughters have birthdays, we try to invite everyone.

There is no holiday where it seems we don't have someone over to grill out or swim or play games.

Scripture makes it pretty obvious that Jesus' command to keep an open house is part of how I am to live as His follower. It seems like it should be in our DNA as Christians. Jesus was always talking about celebrations and inviting people to the party, and most of the time, it was the unexpected people. In Luke 15:5–7, Jesus told a parable about one lost sheep: "And when he finds it, he joyfully puts it on his shoulders and goes home. Then he calls his friends and neighbors together and says, 'Rejoice with me; I have found my lost sheep.' I tell you that in the same way there will be more rejoicing in heaven over one sinner who repents than over ninety-nine righteous persons who do not need to repent." Imagine for a moment that they had a party for *you* in heaven when you came to Jesus. That's right. The second you committed your life to Christ, heaven threw a "rager" in your honor. That is something! I wonder if there is a team of professional partiers in heaven. Do they have an emcee? A heavenly hype man? Who is the house band for those kinds of events? I wonder if they have a whole army of event-planning angels that work round the clock to prepare celebrations just for us. That means that God thinks you are a big deal, doesn't it?

But Jesus didn't stop with the party stuff there. He told another story about a prodigal son who took all the money from his dad's inheritance and ran away. While he was gone, he spent every dime of that inheritance money, got himself into all kinds of trouble, and finally decided that he would have it much better back at his dad's place, even if he went back to work as a servant.

The son returned home with his tail between his legs. Jesus said when the father saw his son while he was still a long way off, "the father said to his servants, 'Quick! Bring the best robe and put it on him. Put a ring on his finger and sandals on his feet. Bring the fattened calf and kill it. Let's have a feast and celebrate'" (Luke 15:22–23). It's important to note that in that day and time, for the son to ask for his father's inheritance would've been a huge insult—it was like saying that he wished his dad were dead! But even after everything the son had done, the father showered him with presents and a robe and threw a big celebration! Jesus was trying to get through to His listeners in this story how much God loves us. It doesn't sound like God wants us to be too hard on ourselves, does it? He's the God who stays with wide open arms, isn't He? No matter where we have been or what we have done, there is a party waiting for us if we will simply come home to Him.

Perhaps now you are getting the picture that the kingdom of God involves a lot of partying. And yet Jesus told another story in the book of Matthew to remind us about the type of people who take part in His kingdom. He talked about the ruler who was throwing a banquet, and the usual folks everyone assumed should attend didn't even bother to show up. They apparently had more important things going on. So, this king told his servants, "'Go to the street corners and invite to the banquet anyone you find.' So the servants went out into the streets and gathered all the people they could find, the bad as well as the good, and the wedding hall was filled with guests" (Matt. 22:9–10). The folks who showed up were the ones who were simply ready to accept the invitation. I want to be a person who lives with my heart open to God's invitation to celebrate like that too.

A Celebration, Not an Obligation

Parents of younger kids may have read the children's book *If You Give a Pig a Party*. It's about balloons and friends and a big sleepover. It's a fun book that makes you remember that there isn't a party without a community. Sometimes I think we need to get a little bit better about the balloons and the celebrations we have when we gather in Jesus' name. We need more cake at church gatherings. More singing. Maybe more dancing. Jesus was always attending dinner parties. He was always at the center of a group of sinners and disreputable people. He showed up to party with the people who needed Him the most.

Not every church service needs to look like David's celebration in front of the ark. But too often when we get together in Jesus' name and call it church, it ends up looking more like a solemn ceremony than one of the celebrations Jesus talked about in His parables. What if we celebrated each week in the same way they celebrate in heaven each time someone gives their life to Jesus? What if the world could say, "Wow, those Christians really know how to throw a party!" What if the invitation to church was an invite to a celebration? I love to make every Matthew West band performance a fun celebration. I love to bring the laughter and the energy and excitement. We go to church at my concerts. But our church is a party. I want us to be better at having church like that! And even more so, I want my life off the stage and outside of the church to continue to radiate the joy I have in Christ. When you walk with a God who loves you, every day should be knitted together by joy. Even when Jesus wasn't teaching and even when He wasn't going to dinner, He still seemed to find Himself at the center of the party. And who better to be at the center of the party than the guy who brings the punch, right?

I always find it compelling that Jesus chose to kick off His first miracle at a celebration. I love the wedding story because Jesus attended this event with His disciples, and the Gospel of John tells us right away that His mom was there. It's the first time Jesus' mom and the disciples are mentioned in the same place. Now, this brings up all kinds of possible funny scenarios that the Bible doesn't even talk about. I wonder if Jesus' mom met all twelve of the crew at once. What was that introduction like? And was this wedding the first time she met them? Did she feel like my mom probably did when I had a group of high school buddies come rolling into the front door of our house? But one of the best parts of this wedding story is the way that Jesus' mom came to Him about the problem. It is almost like she was telling Him the trash needed to be taken out or the lawn needed to be mowed.

It is such a great scene: "A wedding took place at Cana in Galilee. Jesus' mother was there, and Jesus and his disciples had also been invited to the wedding. When the wine was gone, Jesus' mother said to him, 'They have no more wine.' ['There is a problem, and it's yours, Jesus.'] 'Woman, why do you involve me?' Jesus replied. 'My hour has not yet come.' His mother said

THE GOD WHO STAYS

to the servants, 'Do whatever he tells you'" (John 2:1–5). So, Jesus didn't seem super pleased that His mom asked Him to be involved. Moms everywhere reading this can almost visualize Jesus' expression when she told Him about the problem. And notice that Mary didn't seem to doubt that Jesus would follow through. He told the servants to fill empty jugs up with water. They took them to the master of the wedding banquet. He tasted the water and, lo and behold, it had become wine. And not just any wine—Jesus turned it into the best wine for this wedding party! The head of the party marveled that the best wine had been saved for the end of the party. Jesus was the original one-man party.

The lesson from the wedding miracle is that Jesus is going to take care of you. Jesus didn't push back on His mom and say that the party wasn't important. He made sure that the head of the party wouldn't run out of drinks. I think God wants us to be present and celebrate the award, the ceremony, the success. For me, part of learning to celebrate what God is doing in my life is simply letting go and trusting that He is going to take care of the details. Because He always comes through! When God throws a party, you aren't going to run out of the essentials. And guess what is essential at a party? Joy. After all, it is kind of difficult to live a life of joy when you are full of anxiety and worry.

My friend Bob organizes something called Lifest. It is a weekend festival that first launched in Oshkosh, Wisconsin, and is now also in Nashville. This festival is a highlight of every summer. The Cheeseheads of Wisconsin know how to throw a party. I love Bob and his vision for this event. He calls it a "party with a purpose." I love that. It sounds like something we should all adopt in our daily lives if we follow Jesus. When God throws a party, it is never the awkward junior high dance where everyone is standing on the sidelines like wallflowers, the boys and girls separated and three people dancing while the principal looks on. No, I think it looks a lot like Lifest. People are dancing and singing and moving together in celebration. I wonder sometimes if our church gatherings really reflect the level of joy we should have in our lives. I want church to be like that for me. I want it to have all the key ingredients for a party. A true celebration, not an obligation.

Being Joyful in Hope and Drive-By Birthdays

When I talk about the joy in our hearts, I don't mean the temporary emotion of happiness. Happiness is transient because it is dependent on our circumstance. Joy is grounded in the eternal presence of God. Joy holds a place in our hearts even when there aren't balloons and confetti anywhere to be found. Joy is the deep assurance that sustains us even when the outcomes aren't going our way. Paul wrote that we should "be joyful in hope" (Rom. 12:12). Now, when Paul wrote this it was from firsthand experience because he had already faced some tough times. "Joyful in hope" is like saying "joyful in the not-yet." Joyful before the breakthrough.

I was so moved when I met a new friend in Maryland whose spouse had just passed away because of COVID-19. She and her husband loved to attend my concerts together whenever we played close enough for them to go. She told me that she was there that evening to celebrate her husband's life. It was one of those moments in my profession that I'll never forget. She was living "joyful in hope" in a way that impacted my own faith. The fact that she came to my concert to celebrate that she will see her husband again someday is such a deep truth about the assurance of Christ's joy that sustains us. It is an unspeakable joy that carries us through the good times and the hard times. It is there in the wins and the losses. In the beauty of new life and the grief over loved ones whom we will see again someday. What a party that will be!

There were many lonely moments during quarantine that made us feel separated from our communities and discouraged. My wife, Emily, is such a people person. She is always our party thrower and social organizer. Since I knew she was really missing our friends in that long stretch during the 2020 lockdown, I planned a special surprise birthday party for her. In a time when we couldn't gather with other people, it was going to take some real creativity. I was able to pull off something epic with balloons and cake (of course) and friends and everything she could ever want. I tied up balloons outside the house and had her sit in a chair next to the driveway. For the next hour, we had all her friends drive by in their cars with the windows down, singing and waving and laughing in one big, long parade. There were no hugs and there wasn't any dancing (and no naked nephews), but it was still an epic celebration. In the middle of the tough times, I threw a birthday party for her that she says she will never forget.

One of my favorite memories of that season of our lives is Emily sitting in that chair watching a long line of dear friends drive by with tears of joy and gratitude rolling down her cheeks.

Joy isn't found in perfect conditions and situations. And it's not found just in the four walls of a church building. Sometimes when things get tough, it is easier to lean in and locate the joy. It is easier to appreciate the party. Why? Because we must focus a little bit harder on gratitude. We have to seek out the joy. Pursue the party. What if we train our hearts to look for the joy, to look for ways to join the party, no matter what our circumstances are? I wonder if that is what Paul was writing about when he said to "be joyful in hope." Maybe it is how our hearts are oriented. Jesus came to bring us joy in the here and now, not just in heaven. And that means we can find it in all circumstances. I am not talking about being "fake happy" or smiling when you don't feel like it. Real joy is different. It cuts through the heaviness of this life and gives you the deep sense that even when things are tough, you could run naked toward the nearest swimming pool because you still have your breath and God is still with you. Real joy is knowing that because of the resurrection, no matter what life brings us, the end of the story is that everything will be set right.

The Birthday Dance and the Joy of Perfect Gifts

I've explained how birthdays are a big deal in the West family and how these traditions began way back with my parents. We take those celebrations very seriously. There is a ritual in the West house called "The Birthday March." We gather as many of the West clan together as we can fit into one room and sit the birthday person of honor on a chair. Everyone begins to march around the birthday person in a circle and sing "Happy Birthday" until my dad yells out, "Crescendo!" That's the signal for the energy of the celebration to go up a notch! We all begin to march faster and faster and sing louder and louder. Now, during this whole routine, the marchers are also busy piling the birthday gifts onto the guest of honor's lap until we cannot even see the person anymore because the presents are stacked so tall. It is the kind of celebration that everyone looks forward to. We show up for it and, like it says in the Bible, "rejoice over you with singing" (Zeph. 3:17).

Recently, my friend was bedridden with the coronavirus for over a month. He is a busy dad of four and runs his own business, but he literally couldn't even get up to make himself food during that time. Interestingly, he now talks about how God's gifts were so real to him in those difficult moments. The sound of his daughter singing and running up and down the stairs outside his room. Hearing his three sons playing ball in the backyard. Listening to his wife's laughter. Even during those scary moments, he felt like God was piling presents onto his lap. When he recounted that experience to me, it made me wonder how often we allow ourselves to sit before God's Birthday March like that. And how often are we so busy that we miss appreciating the gifts right in front of us? Henry van Dyke was an English professor at Princeton University who found himself so overwhelmed by the splendor of a mountain view in Massachusetts that he wrote the song "Joyful, Joyful We Adore

Thee." He simply took time to notice the gifts of God's creation, and it led to one of the most popular hymns of all time. I want to be more intentional about noticing the beauty that God has placed in my life. I want to learn to be joyful for the presents He is piling on my lap each day.

I believe that learning to accept God's perfect gifts will fill us with the joy we need to pass those gifts on to the world. When you realize that your life is an experience of God dancing around your chair and gifting you until you can't hold any more, how can you not freely do that for other people? I think that is what it truly means when we say that our cup is running over. Every good and perfect gift truly comes from God. The gift of Jesus, the forgiveness of sins, and eternity in heaven! That is true joy. It's like the feeling you have when you give someone the perfect gift, the very thing that they would never buy for themselves. Joy is knowing in your heart that God loves to shower gifts on you just like that. He is gifting you right now with each moment and each breath that you take. Your life is like a perfect surprise party. Jesus said that His joy would be in us (John 15:11). He commanded us to love each other as He has loved us. He wants us to pass on His joy and welcome others to His party. God wants us to serve others with that kind of joy in our hearts. He promises that He will be with us in the good times and the bad, and He sustains us with joy through all the seasons of life. Jesus is the source of that joy, joy, joy, joy down in our hearts. Now, if you'll excuse me, Marty the One-Man Party has some celebrating to do. I'm sure there's some cake around here somewhere.

[CHAPTER 9]

God Stays on the Move

The Original Mover and Shaker

I firmly believe that those long days when we found ourselves quarantined inside our homes; hidden away from in-person meetings; social distanced from dinners, conversations, and hugs with friends; and living in a constant state of six feet of separation were anything but meaningless or lost. It turns out a season of stress and anxiety or a worldwide pandemic will make you ask the question "Where is God?" with a little bit of desperation. I've never particularly cared for that word, *desperation*. If it were a train station, it would be just one stop short of *hopeless*. Too needy. Too revealing. And who wants to admit that they feel desperate? Don't we pride ourselves on self-sufficiency? Desperation is the opposite of confidence. Now, there's a word. *Confidence.* I would much rather project confidence than desperation.

But with nowhere to go and no one to see, the need to project confidence can subside and the reality of the gift of desperation can finally be received. I am discovering that when it comes to my spiritual life, desperation isn't always such a bad thing. Those moments when I'm shaking my head at the news and wondering what in the world God is doing train my heart to look a little closer. It turns out that when the world was forced to hit the pause button, it created some space and time for a kind of desperate reflection. And when you're desperate you tend to lean in, listen closely, and look up.

A Sunday God in a Monday Through Saturday World

Difficult times have a way of returning our attention to what is most important in life. Those days forced me to be still before the Lord, so that I could know He is God. And the season of stillness helped open my eyes to God's motion in the world. It was a little bit like when I am out on my morning run and have to pause near the side of the road at a light and watch the moving cars speed by; thirty miles an hour seems so much faster when you aren't driving alongside them. Or if you're a child of the eighties like me, maybe you once found a spot near the airport to watch planes take off. As you watched from the hood of your car, you experienced the energy of that huge, winged machine launching into the sky in a way you can't feel when you are sitting inside the plane. Somehow, our stillness can highlight the power and speed of the movement around us that we miss when we are on the move. In the same way, something about slowing my pace and allowing my heart to be still helped me recognize the powerful ways that God was moving. It opened my heart to the prayers and praises rolling through my social feeds each week. In my stillness, I saw God's redemptive motion through the world.

When I was a young pastor's kid growing up in Downers Grove, Illinois, I believed that God was contained to Sundays. Maybe you did too. My Sunday God went to work at 10:00 a.m., basking in the safe glow of the stained-glass light, surrounded by people dressed in their Sunday best, with the familiar cadence of Dad's sermons, hymns, and altar calls. But then I met God on a blue couch in my parents' basement on a random weekday afternoon. Not in a church building. Not on a Sunday. It was an off-schedule appearance by God. Nothing "set the scene," except an unexpected television sermon. God surprised me by showing up when I had planned on watching Ryne Sandberg and my Cubs lose on a nice afternoon at Wrigley. It was my first lesson that God moves whenever and wherever and however He chooses.

To Expect the Unexpected

Of course, as I grew older, I began to see the truth that God's presence is anywhere that two or more are gathered in His name. God didn't need a formal sanctuary. His presence wasn't connected to a worship leader with skinny jeans and tattoos, or a hipster preacher with a gourmet, ethically sourced coffee bar in the lobby. He didn't need any of that to pave the way for His arrival. He'd show up in the basement of a frat house party. At a prison concert or a state fair. While I've definitely witnessed God move in powerful ways inside of a church building, I also know that God does a lot of His best work beyond church property lines. If we believe His reach ends as we turn out of our church driveway, we are missing out. One of the biggest lessons I have learned as I've traveled is that the whole world is God's sanctuary. I see Him showing up in unexpected places and in unexpected ways.

In a time when I was focused on the fundamentals of drawing closer to God—during a season of physical separation from my blue couch locked away in a storage unit—I was reminded that it is human nature to always want to limit God to a particular place. In other words, after we have a God experience on a blue couch, we often try to keep Him on a blue couch. Keeping God in church, on Sundays, around the people who look and talk like us, makes Him a little less wild and a little more manageable. Maybe it feels safer and easier for us to understand how God moves when we can confine God to one place. And maybe, if we're being honest, confining God to one place and time is something we do to try to keep other parts of our lives free from the invasion of a God who might have other plans. Do I like a Sunday God because it leaves Monday through Saturday up to me to move as I see fit? Do I prefer a Sunday God because deep down I know I'm a Sunday Christian?

The Bible tells us that when God "moved into the neighborhood," as *The Message* version phrases it (John 1:14), He did it in a completely different way than anyone would assume the God of the universe would choose to enter human history. Instead of showing up in all the power and glory He could muster, which is what you and I would probably do, He arrived as an innocent and helpless baby. When He could've easily been born into a royal family in the most lavish palace in the world, He chose to be born to a scandalously wed young couple in a simple manger surrounded by stinky livestock. And of all the cities that He could've chosen as His hometown, He picked a remote, one-stoplight kind of village that was so far out in the country that people probably had to ask, "So, where is that again?" It seems like Jesus was letting us know from His arrival that we should expect the unexpected.

God Is on the Move—Kind of Like the A-Team

Traveling across the country on a tour really opens your eyes to the amazing things that God is doing at every stop. Touring has become like a check-in with God's work. When we are all crammed onto that bus, my dad, who is our "tour pastor," will read Scripture and give us a short message and bring us together in prayer. We take a moment and set aside the pizza and turn off the football game and ask my dad to "get our eyes on Jesus to the best of our ability" before we go out to play a concert. But the most amazing part of our small community devotional session is when Dad shares with us the incredible stories of God moving and working in the lives of the people we meet on tour. He shares stories of people who were at the show the night before. A security guard shared with Dad that he had been having suicidal thoughts and the concert really spoke to him. Hearing how God was moving the night before in the city we just left fires us up to hit the stage the next night filled with anticipation to see how He will move again. We pray before every show that it is more than just a concert, that lives are changed, hurts are healed, burdens are lifted—not because of the band, but because of the presence of Jesus. It is an incredible reminder that God is moving in amazing ways in every city we visit.

The way I see God work as I travel from place to place reminds me a little bit of how the A-Team from the 1980s TV show went about their heroic business. They were rule breakers, always nomadic and one step ahead of the authorities, but always doing good work for the people who had nowhere else to turn. I loved those characters: B.A., Face, Murdock, and Hannibal. Each episode began with the statement, "If you have a problem, if no one else can help . . . maybe you can hire the A-Team." If you're a little bit older than me, you might remember Caine from the famous 1970s television show *Kung Fu*. He would walk from town to town, arriving just in time to save the day for people in the toughest circumstances. I think Jesus moves in the same way and looks to help the same kind of people with nowhere else to turn.

There is a great moment in the Bible where Jesus met up

with a big-time religious leader named Nicodemus under the cover of night. Nicodemus was a Pharisee who wanted to talk to Jesus about the kingdom of God. In the conversation about what it means to be born again, Jesus told him, "The wind blows wherever it pleases. You hear its sound, but you cannot tell where it comes from or where it is going. So it is with everyone born of the Spirit" (John 3:8). Jesus explained to Nicodemus how God works in the world. I think He was highlighting how God's Spirit moves like the wind. He isn't static or predictable. God isn't tied to a place, a circumstance, a certain space, or the right conditions. He is always on the move.

When I read through the Gospels, I notice that Jesus was always moving. He was always traveling from town to town. He didn't set up shop in Nazareth or Galilee or Jerusalem and just let everyone come to Him, even though He probably could have. He hit the road. He walked toward the disciples and said, "Come and *follow* Me." He was calling them to move some-where. He performed incredible miracles as He traveled from place to place. A sick woman touched His cloak and was healed as He was on His way. He cast out demons on the way. He healed lepers on the way. He gave a blind man sight on the way. Most of His work wasn't done in synagogues (which were the churches of the day). Kind of like the A-Team or Caine from *Kung Fu*, Jesus was constantly on the road to rescue people from sin, sickness, and oppression. Not only that, but Jesus didn't always follow the rules. He healed people during the Jewish Sabbath. He ate meals with questionable people. He spent time with Gentiles. He was innovative in His movement of love. I am learning that God still works that way in the world. God moves in unexpected ways. Sometimes what He is doing looks like a crooked path. Sometimes it is confusing. Things often look confusing and crooked to those who can't see what the innovator sees, and God is the great Innovator.

A Different Kind of Mover and Shaker

If you open your eyes to what is happening in the world, you will see that God is really into innovation. During the pandemic, when we couldn't meet in person, churches across the country were put in a tough position about how to provide a space and a platform for people to worship safely. And it was also challenging to figure out ways for churches to continue impacting their neighborhoods. But I witnessed faith organizations and churches everywhere pivot and get creative about how they could make an impact. I began to take part in virtual church services that had a new sense of urgency and importance. It was amazing. I could play to thousands of worshipers in California and then twenty minutes later play for folks in Texas, all in one Sunday morning from my Story House studio. Every time I went live on social media for fifteen minutes of Quiet Time, I walked away with thousands of prayer requests, praises, and the knowledge that the community of God was really coming together from their couches and homes to worship and lift up one another in prayer. Where two or more gather, even virtually, God moves. It was clear to me that God was on the move even while His people were locked in their homes and physically couldn't go anywhere.

I witnessed how God moves unexpectedly—just as Jesus told Nicodemus, "The wind blows wherever it pleases"—when I had eighty-seven concerts (re)moved from my schedule during that season. However, God used that time to connect me with people in ways that couldn't have happened if I'd been out on the road playing for those months. Not that I didn't have some depressed moments thinking about not being on the road, but if I would have been traveling and playing those eighty-seven concert dates, there wouldn't have been the space or energy for the new podcast that has connected me to the stories that have revealed so much of God's work. I wouldn't have had the time to pour more energy into my nonprofit organization, popwe. And I wouldn't have the relationship with the thousands of people who want to worship and pray for one another each Wednesday morning on social media.

Whatever situation we face, God moves in magnificent and unexpected ways that can look a little strange to the world. Sometimes God on the move looks like marching around Jericho a bunch of times just blowing trumpets. Sometimes it looks like Jesus stopping for a moment next to a sycamore tree. Sometimes it looks like Gideon sending most of his army home right before a big battle. It can look like Israel marching to the shore of the Red Sea where they appeared to be trapped. Or even Jesus choosing the very disciple who would deny Him three times to be the founder of His church. It is almost like God *enjoys* finding new and innovative ways to do His work in our lives. And isn't it fascinating that He chooses to move in directions that defy logic and look strange to the world? God's work seems to be the antithesis of the "movers and shakers" of the world today.

The world stands up and applauds people like Bezos, Musk, Winfrey, or Gates. The people with the biggest social followings or the most money get all the front-page press and adoration. But if we are going to follow the way Jesus moves in the world, we need to remember that He was the opposite of the world's version of a mover and shaker. In fact, any time Jesus had the chance to prove Himself as worthy in terms of what the world valued, He actively avoided it. Instead of having a "take-a-selfie" victory moment when He healed people, He mostly hushed them and told them to go home and not tell anyone. Instead of defending Himself to Pilate, He stayed quiet. Instead of riding into Jerusalem like the conquering hero the Jewish people were all expecting the Messiah to be, He chose the path of the cross. Instead of building social capital, He chose to have eternal influence.

Moved by a Jesus Hippie and My Friend Ron

Several years ago, the band had the chance to fly to California for some big concerts. We arrived in San Francisco and were going to perform that evening on a huge stage at a music festival. After landing at the airport, our bleary-eyed band was greeted by our driver, who helped us load our gear into a van. My conversation with the driver in that van on the way to the venue ended up being the most memorable part of the trip. He looked like a poster child for hippie culture straight out of a Woodstock documentary or a 1960s photo album. He was wearing a tie-dyed T-shirt, blue jeans, and well-worn Chuck Taylors and had a bandanna around his head. He had a thick beard and long, unruly hair that had gone gray. You get the picture. He was the real deal.

As we began to talk, he handed me a guitar pick with his name on it and told me he was a musician. While he drove the band to our show, he shared that God had called him to play music for the people of the Haight-Ashbury neighborhood. He was passionate about ministering to the homeless, the people with mental health issues, and the lost. Every evening, he would take his guitar and set up on the same street corner to sing his Jesus songs for the people who lived there. It struck me as we rode on to that big stage that this committed musician was participating in God's "moving into the neighborhood" there in San Francisco. This hippie, Jesus-loving folk singer was unconcerned with being a mover and shaker in the world. He didn't go on tour or have a greatest hits album. He wasn't concerned with record deals or sound checks. He just focused on sharing the gospel with the people who needed it the most. And his Jesus songs were part of God's movement toward us on our visit to California. His testimony helped me remember why I do what I do. It also reminded me that God's moves will never look like success in the eyes of the world.

And that is the thing—God isn't just moving in unexpected and random ways in the world; if you look a little closer, you will see that He is always moving *toward* us. And He often uses us to help Him move toward others. I know just as He used the blue couch moment to change my life as a teenager, God also used the literal locking away of my blue couch in a storage unit to move toward me. He has used this season of quiet and solitude to highlight the six feet of separation I had created from Him. I believe He is always working and moving to close that gap between us.

I felt God moving toward me one day when I met a guy named Ron. Ron had reached out to popwe to share his story and in the hopes of having a message relayed to me. Ron was in the final days of his battle with ALS. Hospice care had been called in and he knew his time on earth was coming to an end. He wanted to let me know that every morning he requested that his hospice nurses start the day with one song as they helped him get ready for the day. My song. A song called "Strong Enough" was Ron's anthem. It's a song that echoes the promise of Philippians 4:13: "I can do all this through him who gives me strength." I was so moved by this story that I reached back out to Ron and we set up a Zoom call to meet each other. I planned to play Ron's song for him and prayed that God might use me to encourage Ron for a few moments. What I didn't expect was that Ron had other plans for our Zoom call. He spent the entire time encouraging *me*. With his nurses by his side, he fought for every word, but he made every word count. "Matthew, God is using you! Matthew, God is so proud of you! Matthew, keep it up! Your best music is ahead of you!"

I sat there in tears because what Ron didn't know was that at that moment in time, I was in the depths of my own personal discouragement. I was completely depressed and desperate to know that God was still moving. Of course, Ron had no way of knowing that. But there he was, using some of his last words in the last days of his life to lift me up. God moved me to write a song called "Strong Enough," which moved a guy named Ron who was battling ALS to remember the One who gave him strength. And God moved Ron to reach out to me. And now God has moved me to tell Ron's story in the hopes that it just might move you. Did you catch all that? Because God's moving is always there—it only requires that we pay attention to notice Him.

A few weeks later I received the call that Ron had gone home to be with Jesus. Ron had moved home. And my life is forever changed by a Zoom call with my friend. I wrote a song about Ron days after the news that he had passed. It's called "Wonderful Life":

> *It'll send you flying high*
> *It'll bring you to your knees*
> *It's the heartbreak and the happiness*
> *And everything between*
> *It's the laugh until it hurts*
> *It's the hurt until you cry*
> *Can't have one without the other*
> *It's how you know that you're alive*
> *In this broken and beautiful, gone mad and magical*
> *Awfully wonderful life*

God isn't just moving toward us; He is also always urging us to move if we will pay attention. The moments I've found myself the most discouraged about my life are when I am stuck at home with my head under my pillow. They are the times when I have nothing to do but flip on the television, scroll mindlessly through social media, or play another game of Candy Crush. But when God is moving me, it is a lot more exciting than a prompting to move to the kitchen pantry so that I can eat more potato chips! We see all through the Bible that Jesus wants to move us in meaningful ways, from the dead spaces in our lives to an eternal way of living. We've talked about how God stays away from the safe spaces, but if we are going to meet Him where He is at work, we have to be willing to be moved by Him.

In Acts 9, Paul (Saul) was out on the road hunting down Christians when he was suddenly struck blind and heard the voice of Jesus calling to him. He was baptized into the faith, given his sight back, and began preaching that Jesus is the Messiah. Jesus gave him a new life; he went from persecuting Christians to building the church around the world. Paul didn't sit around and waste time; he moved into action. He went on four mission trips, traveling and preaching from city to city: Jerusalem, Caesarea, Corinth, Damascus, Ephesus, Philippi, and Rome, just to name a few. And his ministry helped spread the gospel all over the world. Even in the face of the beatings and imprisonment along his journey, he wrote, "I consider that our present sufferings are not worth comparing with the glory that will be revealed in us" (Rom. 8:18). Because of Jesus, Paul became a man on the move.

And as we allow God to move us, we should do it in the confidence that wherever we are going, He is already there at work. God's movement in the world is omnipresent; He is operating in all places at the same time. He calls us to participate in His movement, not the other way around.

I had a real-life *Planes, Trains, and Automobiles* experience (except boats were used as well) on a visit to Panama with Operation Christmas Child that reminded me of how God is moving everywhere. In one trip I traveled by plane to Panama City, then by bus for a couple of hours to a remote village, which is where I thought our journey would end. But I was wrong. Our group was then loaded into two small boats that took us across a river. Once on the other side of the river, we walked uphill before finally arriving at our destination. Each change in transportation took me further away from comfort and safety.

It took a lot of different vehicles and a ton of miles to get there. As we finally arrived at this remote village, it dawned on me that God will go to great lengths to move us to participate in what He is doing. In one day, we had covered so much distance to be with these children. And the best part was that when we arrived, we were surprised to find that our visit was probably more life-changing for us than for the children we had traveled there to see. I spent the day with a pastor's child in this poverty-stricken part of the world who opened my eyes to how God was moving in that village ahead of our arrival. When you just open yourself up to being moved, no matter how, no matter what the mode of transportation, He will take you where He needs you the most—and it isn't always halfway around the world. Sometimes He is just moving me into my own studio.

Those pandemic months away from the road moved me to a different kind of microphone, which provided a window to the work that God was doing around the world. I went from the fast pace of traveling to sitting in the stillness of my studio with a front-row seat to the power of God's motion. Each week, I began to hear how God was moving incredible people into action on my podcast. I met with Alex Kendrick, who faithfully moved forward with the kind of stories he believed in, even though they were rejected time after time by Hollywood executives. Can you imagine sitting down with some Hollywood producers and explaining that the movie you wanted to make was about an elderly woman who prays in her closet? But that was exactly what God was moving Alex to do. Of course, Alex persevered, God moved mountains, and Alex was able to get the film *War Room* made, and it was a huge success. It was a dominant force at the box office when it came out in 2015.

I learned how God moved Lathan Warlick, a hip-hop artist from Jackson, Tennessee, to start creating inspirational music. Lathan explained how he came face-to-face with a .45-caliber pistol in a fight at a dance club in 2011. God moved him from that near-death experience to leave his career and to create life-giving music that points his listeners toward important messages about God's love and unity. And I also got him to come record the song "What If" with me!

I met Olivia Lane, a talented songwriter who lost her voice and almost her life. But God moved toward her in the middle of that crisis and transformed her life. She left behind her life as an atheist to become a believer.

I was able to spend time talking with my friends Mack and Meredith Brock about their greatest passion. Mack is a worship leader and a songwriter, and Meredith is a literary agent. But God moved them to become foster parents and advocates for children. They talked about how saying yes to moving with God has changed their lives and the lives of the children they care for in their home.

The reality is that if we are following Jesus and if we are listening for His voice, He is always moving us somewhere, toward someone or something. We are called to be people of the Way who are on the way. We only need to say yes to moving through life by following the Mover. In the Bible, people were moved to Jesus—then moved *by* Jesus. And when we are moved by Jesus, we begin to move like Him—and that is the kind of life that is truly infectious to other people!

How Can I Move with God?

God doesn't just move us and move toward us; He moves *with* us. I am so thankful that I have gotten the chance to hear the stories of God's work from the people I've met while touring. I can tell you about Cindy, who would bring her mom to our concerts. Cindy's mom, Carolyn, was blind. She couldn't see me, but I could see her in the front row with a big smile on her face, worshiping God right alongside her daughter. Cindy's mom passed away last year. Not long after, Cindy showed up at one of my concerts. Her mom had bought her tickets to that concert and made her promise she would attend for the both of them no matter what happened. During the concert, I looked into the crowd and saw Cindy and thought about the seat next to her where her mom would have been. I prayed that this concert would be a celebration of life in the middle of Cindy's season of grief. Experiences like these have helped me realize that I am stepping into the memories of the people who attend my shows, and they are stepping into mine. God moving with me shows up in the faces and stories of the people I play for and the people who lift me up with their testimony of God's faithfulness. He is moving with us and through us even when we don't recognize it.

The Gospel of Matthew calls Jesus "Immanuel," which means "God with us." Immanuel means that Jesus isn't just with us some of the time or in the right circumstances. It means He is with us in every breath and in every moment. And He is moving whenever and wherever I take the time to look around and notice. I took that blue couch on tour from concert to concert with me for a long time. Sometimes, I still do. I like to joke that the Matthew West show carried that Wayfair couch the same way the Israelites carried the ark from place to place. But I bought that set piece and put it on stage to represent that catalyst moment that we have when God moves in our lives. I used it to remind myself of how the Holy Spirit moved in my life. It was an ever-present reminder on the road that God is with me wherever I go. Deep down, I want to be moved like I was on that blue couch each and every day.

I want to be part of how God is moving in the world. I want to be awake enough to participate in His movement to redeem all of creation. I want to learn how to still my heart, to be prayerful, and to focus my attention on Him so that I can be part of that holy motion. And I want to be willing to allow Him to move into my neighborhood—every part of it.

So, what direction do I need to move to join Him in what He is already doing today? How can I let Him move me right now? And how is Immanuel moving with me, before me, and behind me this very moment? What if I truly embrace those moments of stillness and prayer each day and look at the world at large to see how God is in motion? What if God is moving in the middle of my victories? What if God is moving in the devastation of a diagnosis, job loss, or even our grief? What if even when it feels like we are at a standstill—that the world is at a standstill—God is still moving? And what if the choice to be still is the only way to see where God is moving me next? Whether it's a Zoom call with a stranger or a journey to a remote village in the middle of nowhere, all I know is, life gets good when I move where God is moving me. And I don't want to miss where He's moving me next.

[CHAPTER 10]

God stays the same

New "Normals" but Always the Same God

Remember how you felt when you walked out of a skate rink, arcade, or movie theater into the midday sunshine when you were a kid? Despite the lessons taken from this recent season, I feel like we are all squinting into the sun, tentatively and gingerly moving forward with our lives after what we've been through. I've also noticed that there seems to be a lingering, uneasy feeling among people, as though they're waiting for the other shoe to drop. It's like those moments in the scary movie when you know the bad guy is there and you're watching the unsuspecting teenagers laughing and hanging out, not realizing the danger they're in. Mixed in with all this apprehension we now have is also the exhale and joy of gathering, playing live music again, hugging, worshiping together, cheering on our teams—just being in the same space with other people. It feels like we held our breath for a long time.

Yes, we've been through it. A long season in the wilderness. It reminds me of C. S. Lewis's description of Narnia at the beginning of *The Lion, the Witch, and the Wardrobe*: "always winter and never Christmas."[1] And I've noticed that the conversations in media and on talk shows and news articles have continued to use the ominous phrases like "in these uncertain times." My favorite is the expression that I've heard people say five million times in these past months: "Well [dramatic pause for effect], I guess this is the *new normal*!" How many times have you heard that on a Zoom call? On a phone conversation with a friend? At a school board meeting? And it is usually said with a tone of resigned defeat, right? As I have focused on getting back to the fundamentals of my faith, I've developed my own idea of what the new normal means for me.

The Times Are Always Changing

The very idea of "normal" is interesting anyway because all our times have been uncertain since the very first moments after God came looking for Adam and Eve and they ran away to hide from Him. That choice made from guilt and shame and their exodus from the safety of the garden pushed them from a life of intimacy with God into a world filled with uncertainty. I'm not really a history buff, but if you do a quick Google search of the twentieth century, you'll read about a worldwide pandemic in 1918, complete with black-and-white photos of people wearing masks at Yankees games in New York. You'll read about the World Wars and the Great Depression and the Holocaust and natural disasters and worse. We live in a broken, fallen world that has always been anything but normal. Isn't it interesting to consider the truth that no matter what we face in the coming years, there will be people who have faced similar circumstances before? Times like these have always been "times like these." It seems that uncertainty is about the only thing we can be certain about in the world.

Several years ago, I spent my summer in Colorado. Whenever the topic of the weather came up, the locals would tell me with a smile, "If you don't like the weather here, just wait around a minute." But as a traveling musician, I've learned that people say this in every region and every city of America! If you don't like the weather in Florida, just wait a minute. If you don't like the weather in Dallas, just give it a minute. There isn't "normal" when it comes to weather. No matter where you live, it is in constant change. But that is the thing about this world that we live in, isn't it? Everything can change in an instant. One minute I am at a sound check. The next minute a worldwide pandemic has shut down everything. The old Bob Dylan tune rings out a great truth about the reality of life—the times certainly are always changing. Our politicians change. Our circumstances change. Our moods, our relationships, our health, our financial status, our choices, our behavior, and other people's opinions of us all change. But as I said before, I am looking upward to a different kind of "new normal."

I've spent most of this wilderness season remembering the One I can really count on. Is there anything in this life or in this world that we can be certain of enough to stand on without fear of it shifting underneath our feet? We may be living in uncertain times in a fallen world that offers promises that it will never keep, but I don't believe that is the true normal that God intended for us. With that thought planted in my mind and the world opening up again, I returned to our storage space as we began to load the bus with equipment to head out for stages across the country. The T-shirts and merchandise boxes came out once more. The mics went hot in front of live audiences again. But there was that first moment, before all the busyness of the business, that moved me deeply. When I opened that warehouse door after over a year, I noticed the replica blue couch sitting in the corner that I had been writing about and thinking about. I walked over and sat down on it in the shadows of that storage space and took a deep breath.

My moment there on the blue couch reminded me of my cab driver's broken-English version of "The God Who Stays." The song that pointed me back to the fundamentals of my faith. It made me realize that I am truly walking into a new kind of normal. I want the fundamentals of my faith to begin with the God who, during all this change, is unchanging. He keeps His promises; He is who He says He is; He always does what He says He will do. In a world that is in constant change, chaos, and turmoil, I want that solid Rock, Immanuel, the Word, His love, His joy to be *my* normal. I want to be living in the awareness of God's faithfulness to me. Sitting on the blue couch in that musty storage space, I was reminded of another great tune from the hymn books of my youth that shaped my love for music—"On Christ, the solid Rock, I stand"—and I began to sing it.[2] How I want that to be my new normal! I want to live my life standing on His promises.

I've Got Air Jordans, but Still No Air

The world we live in makes a lot of empty promises. My journey through writing this book has reminded me that getting back to the fundamentals of faith means trusting that God's Word is His promise to me. There are plenty of words and promises out there to be suspicious about. Think of the words and empty promises that fill your social media feeds every hour via paid advertisements. We are bombarded with messages about what we can look like, what we can do, how much money we can make, and they lead us to chase anything but the One whose promises we can truly count on. Likewise, consider all the promises that have been made by politicians over the years. Wow. In our public relations–savvy culture, it is more and more difficult to trust the guarantees.

I learned a tough lesson about false promises back in my days as a high school basketball player. You recall the Downers Grove junior varsity boys basketball team I mentioned earlier. The team that was only slightly overshadowed by the six-time World Champion Chicago Bulls of the 1990s. I don't think we ever made it on SportsCenter, probably because that Bulls team kept stealing all the Chicago headlines. We didn't even get coverage on "The Ocho" (or ESPN 8, if you've never seen the movie *Dodgeball*)! But that didn't stop me from dreaming of having Stuart Scott or Dan Patrick narrate my own Matthew West highlight. Of course, there were some small challenges to my getting on a highlight reel, one of them being that I couldn't jump quite high enough to dunk.

The solution was obvious to me after watching a few Air Jordan advertisements. The more of Michael Jordan's gear I could wear, the better my chances of dunking. I saved a year's worth of allowance money and mortgaged my future to afford it all, but I finally was able to go to the gym for practice wearing my new Air Jordan shoes, Air Jordan socks, Air Jordan shorts, Air Jordan wristbands, and Air Jordan underwear. I felt legitimately more like the man himself. How could I not while wearing all his Airness's gear? I warmed up for a few minutes jogging up and down in our layup line. I could feel the springs in my shoes. The wings on the Air Jordan insignia even seemed to make me feel lighter on my feet. I was ready. I took the ball and made a running start toward the goal. I jumped, soaring through the air (if only in my mind), and slammed the ball furiously . . . against the bottom of the basketball net. It may have been the closest I ever got to dunking a basketball, about a foot short. To this day, I wonder if having bought the Air Jordan headband would've put me over the top! It is a funny memory, but I think you can identify with being the kid who was sold on the belief that if you just had that one thing, it would make all the difference. You know the promises that we are just one more acquisition, one more pound, one more pay raise away from everything being all right. It's a good thing we grow out of that way of believing—or do we?

Speaking of empty promises, I heard a great story about a pretty famous singer whose manager told him that he needed to lose weight before his next tour. It happens all the time in the entertainment business. The manager bought his artist the Nutrisystem weight loss plan. You've seen those commercials. They promise that you will look just like the former professional athletes and fitness models who are selling it on TV. The manager called his artist the next week to check in on his weight loss progress. The singer raved about it enthusiastically. The food was great, and he was never hungry. There was only one problem. "What's that?" the manager asked. The singer responded, "I haven't received this week's shipment yet." The singer had eaten the entire month's supply of Nutrisystem food in only one week! Sometimes the stuff that the world promises just doesn't work out like it is supposed to. So much for quick fixes. In a world that spins empty words and false promises, it is reassuring to know that God's promises are lasting and true. Jesus tells us that His Word will last forever.

Words on Which to Build Your Life

The Gospel of John begins by talking about Jesus in a much different way than the other Gospels do. John called Jesus "the

Word." He said, "In the beginning was the Word, and the Word was with God, and the Word was God. He was with God in the beginning. Through him all things were made; without him nothing was made that has been made" (John 1:1–3). John told us that Jesus was present at creation, that He is the foundation of everything God made. Then he explained that Jesus was the Word of God made into a human form. The person of Jesus is the manifestation of God's truth from the beginning of time. We lean on the promises of God's Word by following Jesus. When we follow Jesus, we are following the truth, and we learn how to build our lives on that truth through the Bible, which is the Word of God. Pretty straightforward, right?

In the Gospel of Matthew, Jesus took His disciples and a few of His other followers up on a mountain near the Sea of Galilee to do a seminar that Bible scholars named the "Sermon on the Mount." It was like the TED Talk to end all TED Talks. He was teaching them everything they needed to know about the qualities of God's kingdom. It was an incredible instruction manual on how to follow Jesus. During this sermon, Jesus leaned into the question that we all face in this uncertain world: Who can we really trust? He said that "Everyone who hears these words of mine and puts them into practice is like a wise man who built his house on the rock. The rain came down, the streams rose, and the winds blew and beat against that house; yet it did not fall, because it had its foundation on the rock" (Matt. 7:24–25). If we look to Jesus and lean on the promise of His words, we will be able to face all that life can bring us. Jesus continued with a warning of what it looks like if you build your life on the promises of the world. He explained, "everyone who hears these words of mine and does not put them into practice is like a foolish man who built his house on sand. The rain came down, the streams rose, and the winds blew and beat against that house, and it fell with a great crash" (vv. 26–27). On Christ, the solid Rock, I stand. Jesus is the promise I can trust. The Word of God is the only word that truly delivers.

I am learning that God's Word is the antidote to the chaos and empty promises of the world. Our days are filled with so much noise. What does it look like to spend time with God's truth and allow it to grow in my soul? As I get back to the basics, I have asked myself some tough questions, such as, What do I reach for first thing in the morning? Do I open the Bible and fill my heart with God's enduring truth, or do I reach for my phone to scroll through news and advertisements? Do I lean on Jesus to be the same yesterday, today, and tomorrow? Or do I spend my time wringing my hands over the latest unpredictable thing in my life? What if each day I choose to believe the promises of God's Word? What if each day I make a habit to simply say, "Jesus, I trust You because You never change"? I am learning that every time I stand on God's promises, He comes through. He is undefeated. His promises are 100 percent guaranteed. His Word is true, and His love is always faithful.

Faithful Wind in My Sails

A while before the pandemic, Emily and I did a tour together and encouraged couples to join us for a special date night. We called the event "Getaway Night." The idea was simple—it was that every couple needs to be intentional about getting away *with* each other so that we don't wind up wanting to get away *from* each other. Part of the event was a question-and-answer time where Emily and I talked a little bit about our relationship. We shared what's worked for us, what hasn't, the highs and the lows of marriage. And one evening, during that part of the event, Emily gave some advice to the other wives that meant so much to me. She said, "One of the things I try to be intentional about is never giving Matthew a reason to doubt my faithfulness to him. I don't keep phone numbers of old boyfriends. I don't have friendships or relationships with anyone that even comes close to being a sort of gray area. I want him to know that I am faithful to him." I've got to tell you, I didn't know Emily was going to share that, but it was like wind in my sails. I felt ten feet tall as she spoke those words. *My wife loves me! She is faithful to me! She only has eyes for me.* And her faithfulness made me soar with confidence. That moment came back to me recently as I thought about God's fidelity in my life. I am so grateful for Emily and her loving loyalty to me, but no matter how amazing it is, it pales in comparison to the faithfulness of the God who created me. He is the One who will "never leave you nor forsake you" (Deut. 31:8).

The truth of that song "The God Who Stays" has worked its way into my soul this past year as I have worked to truly embrace the themes of this book. When I spend time in God's Word, I see the reflection of God's enduring and faithful love. From the intimacy of those daily walks in the garden of Eden in the cool of the day to the last moment of the Gospels before Jesus' ascension, where He promised, "And surely I am with you always, to the very end of the age" (Matt. 28:20), my heart is moved by the revelation that the entire message of the gospel is a message of pursuit. God is faithfully running in my direction. We talked about the scene in the Gospel of John where the religious leader Nicodemus came to Jesus to ask Him about what it meant to be born again. In their conversation about God's love and faithfulness, the final thing that Jesus told Nicodemus was probably one of the most important truths of the Bible. It is a verse that you've heard mentioned, even if you have never darkened the door of a church. But sometimes hearing words too many times can keep us from really hearing the truth in them.

Jesus told Nicodemus, "For God so loved the world that he gave his one and only Son, that whoever believes in him shall not perish but have eternal life" (John 3:16). Think about those words for a moment and the truth that the promises of God know no limits. None of us, no matter how hard we try, even in our best efforts and intentions, could ever live up to that kind of faithful love in our own words and deeds. To put John 3:16 bluntly: God loves you so relentlessly and so loyally that He voluntarily offered up His one and only Child to be crucified, executed, beaten, spit on, and nailed to a cross, just so that He could be close to you again. Maybe John 3:16 is all about God working on *His* new normal for you. That means that His love is there when we face evil, temptation, illness, and even death. The Bible tells us that God is faithful to complete the work He has begun in each one of us. And the completion of His work in me means that He is always calling me into new life.

One Place God Won't Ever Stay

We've spent the whole book talking about the places that God will always stay. But we can't ignore one big truth of God's love and faithfulness to us. There is, in fact, one place that God refuses to stay. And it is also the one place that He refuses to allow you to stay. No matter who, no matter when, no matter where, God doesn't *ever* stay in the grave. That means that Jesus doesn't stay in sin and death. He always stays out of the darkness. If you miss everything else we have talked about concerning God's love for you, I don't want you to miss this one most consistent thing about God's work in your life: He is always calling you into life!

In some ways, I feel like we are all a little bit like Lazarus from the Bible. He was one of Jesus' good friends and was loved by his sisters Mary and Martha. Jesus was out preaching when He received news of Lazarus's untimely death, but He didn't seem troubled by it. When Jesus finally arrived on the scene, Lazarus had been dead for four days. Jesus told the onlookers to roll the stone away from His friend's tomb. Martha protested, telling Jesus, "by this time there is a bad odor, for he has been there four days" (John 11:39). But Jesus told her that if they simply believed, they would witness God's glory. Before He performed this miracle, Jesus made a few proclamations for the people there at the gravesite, but I believe they are relevant for us to hear today. After the heavy stone was moved away from the tomb, "Jesus looked up and said, 'Father, I thank you that you have heard me. I knew that you always hear me, but I *said this for the benefit of the people standing here, that they may believe that you sent me'"* (John 11:41–42 NKJV, emphasis mine). And then there is the dramatic moment of resurrection: "When he had said this, Jesus called in a loud voice, 'Lazarus, come forth!' The dead man came out, his hands and feet wrapped with strips of linen, and a cloth around his face" (vv. 43–44). But this moment of Jesus calling His friend out of the grave was not yet done. "Jesus said to them, 'Take off the grave clothes and let him go.'" He called Lazarus to life. And He commanded the onlookers to get rid of the wrappings of death that were constricting him from getting back to the business of life!

I think I can hear that call in my own life these days: "Come forth!" Maybe you can too? I imagine Jesus wants us all to shake off our graveclothes, walk from the dead spaces in our lives, and throw off the stuff that weighs us down. In many ways, our lives are like Lazarus's. Jesus is always calling us out toward the light. He doesn't stay in the grave, and He doesn't want us to either. It makes me wonder how I can make a daily habit of shaking my graveclothes off and walking into the light with Jesus. Matthew tells us about Jesus' resurrection: "There was a violent earthquake, for an angel of the Lord came down from heaven and, going to the tomb, rolled back the stone and sat on it" (Matt. 28:2). Then Jesus emerged into the world. "Suddenly Jesus met them. 'Greetings,' he said. They came to him, clasped his feet and worshiped him" (v. 9). The God who stays is the resurrected Jesus, and that is the kind of resurrection life He invites us into no matter who we are, what we have done, or where we have been.

One of my all-time favorite writers is a guy named Brennan Manning. He once described his most famous book, *The Ragamuffin Gospel,* by saying, "It is for the wobbly and weak-kneed who know they don't have it all together. . . . It is for inconsistent, unsteady disciples whose cheese is falling off their cracker."[3] I love that description because I see myself in it. This is exactly who the good news is for! I don't know about you, but Manning's lines make me exhale a little and leave my shoulders feeling lighter. Some days, I think the only consistent thing about me is how inconsistent I am. I started a song a while back that I never finished. I don't know if I ever will. Maybe it is one that was never meant to be finished, but there is a line from it that I find myself singing in moments when I'm keenly aware of my own inconsistencies and brokenness. It goes, "You're my constant; You always stay the same. And Your love never depends on the day." It reminds me of that Brennan Manning line. God's love doesn't stay in darkness, and He is always pulling us toward life. I love how *The Message* version of the Bible calls Jesus the "life-light" that came into the darkness (John 1:1). Jesus is consistent about bringing us out of the grave and delivering us from the dead spaces in life. And His faithfulness is for the "inconsistent, unsteady disciples whose cheese is falling off their cracker"—just like me! If we can only follow the sound of His voice the way Lazarus did, we will find new life. There is no more significant place that God *hasn't* stayed than the grave.

There is a wonderful scene in the Bible where Jesus was sparring with the Sadducees about the character of God and He told them, "God says, 'I am—not was.' . . . The living God defines himself not as the God of dead men, but of the living" (Matt. 22:31–32 MSG). He is the One who is always moving us away from death and toward the things that are eternal. And praise God that His resurrection work in my life is not dependent on my consistency. He is faithfully saying, "Matthew, come forth!" each new day. And I hope that with each new season of life, I am removing more and more of what's weighing me down! Living a resurrection life isn't dependent on us; it is the work of Jesus, and He is the same yesterday, today, and forever. Have you ever considered that maybe "resurrection life" is supposed to be our new normal?

Back to the Blue Couch and into a New Normal

As I sat on that blue couch in that storage unit, for the first time in a very long time I embraced the truth that getting back to the basics of my faith was all about surrender. It is about leaning into the attributes of the God who stays . . . the *same*. The God who stays faithful, patient, and good in a faithless world. He stays attentive even when I have wandered away. I thought about the daily walks that God took with Adam and Eve in the garden in the cool of the day. What if Adam and Eve left *normal* behind when they hid from God? The new normal is the work of the resurrected Jesus to restore that intimate connection between me and my Creator. And nothing can now separate us from Him— not my sins, not my scars, not my failure or my enemies; I am His forever.

I think that kind of kingdom life is God's new normal.

I believe walking with Immanuel is the way I was intended to live. Jesus came to restore that intimacy with God, to bring us back to the same close connection that Adam and Eve had in those walks in the garden. I remember playing the keys of the piano in the Story House and searching out truths about God from the old hymns that led me to the music that I love. Maybe there is no greater hymn than the one that kept resounding through my heart as I prayed prayers of thanksgiving for God's promise through the seasons of my life: "My hope is built on nothing less than Jesus' blood and righteousness . . . On Christ, the solid Rock, I stand, all other ground is sinking sand. All other ground is sinking sand."[4]

You know, there is and will always be uncertainty in the world. From the truth of His Word, we know that we can stand on His promises because God does not change:

> "I the LORD do not change" (Mal. 3:6).
> "But you remain the same, and your years will never end" (Ps. 102:27).
> "'I am the Alpha and the Omega,' says the Lord God, 'who is, and who was, and who is to come, the Almighty'" (Rev. 1:8).

I think for the rest of my life the blue couch is going to mean something a little bit different than it did before all of this. It is no longer just a moment in my past assigned to a certain time and place of my young life like an old, faded Polaroid in a dusty photo album on a shelf. In this life full of constant change, I want my new normal to be that I trust God as my solid Rock. He is the One I can always count on. He is my refuge and my strength and ever-present help in trouble (Ps. 46:1). I am learning to apply the promise that I have been given that Jesus is always there with me. I want to invite you into that promise too. Whenever I think of that blue couch now, it represents not just a moment in time but the enduring love of the God who is with me in all of my moments. Every new morning, every sunrise and sunset, every new breath and every new prayer, every new song can be a blue couch moment because we serve a God who stays the same. A sinner-chasing, prodigal-pursuing, dead-man-raising God who refuses to let us stay in the grave of our sin. I can hear Him calling your name—"Come forth" into the new life and the new normal He is offering to all of us.

[CHAPTER 11]

Being the People Who Stay

A Blue Couch Invitation

When my second album was released, I extended an offer to half a dozen strangers from around the country to visit my childhood home. It's been a few years, but the marketing folks at my record label came up with this homecoming promotional idea to have a radio contest and fly the winners from all over the country to my home city of Chicago. The contest was centered on the major theme of the recording, which was titled *History*. Now, that record also happened to be the first time I ever referenced my blue couch moment (without really talking specifically about the blue couch) in a song called "Next Thing You Know."

So we flew a group of winners to the Windy City and took them to my favorite restaurant downtown. They were able to ride around in our band's bus, and I served as their tour guide to my favorite city. The trip was going to culminate with an intimate concert at my hometown church, the very place where I fell in love with the hymns that would lead me to my love of music. I would perform for the contest winners and a small group from my dad's congregation that weekend. And one of the ideas that the folks at the label suggested was to bring the winners over to visit my childhood home in Downers Grove on the day of the concert. You probably can already guess that there is a blue couch appearance connected to this invitation.

Roping Off Our Blue Couches

Now, I had no idea that my mom was going to do this, but before we had the people over, she really prepared her house for the event. I'll never forget when our tour bus pulled into the driveway of that little blue house there on Janes Avenue. A group of contest winners and I were greeted by my mom and dad waving to us in the front lawn. It was like a suburban version of *The Waltons*. The Wests were all too happy to invite a group of people we'd never met before into the house. A few of them were taking pictures of everything as if it was a tour of Elvis Presley's Graceland, which made me laugh! But little did I know, as we crossed in through the front door, that my mom had turned our home into a full-fledged museum as if it really was Graceland! I found it highly entertaining.

She wrote out descriptions of different meaningful locations around the house and hung them where our visitors could read and learn all about me and my childhood. She also took everyone on a room-by-room guided tour. She was a five-star Airbnb Superhost for those few hours. For the record, Mom has always made her house very comfortable for guests, so the formal signs and museum feel that day wasn't the norm in the West house when we were growing up. It was always a welcoming "come as you are" and "make yourself at home" place where nothing was off-limits. But the tour seemed to be a big hit.

And to this day, I still don't have the words to describe accurately the embarrassment of standing in the hallway as the contest winners took pictures of my childhood bedroom! It felt a little bit like being in the movie *The Truman Show*. Finally, the tour arrived face-to-furniture with the blue couch of my youth. Mom had borrowed some of those things called stanchions (I had to look that word up) with the velvet ropes from a local movie theater and had placed them strategically around the couch to keep people at a safe distance. She had carefully placed a note there that read, "This is where Matthew asked Jesus into his heart." Now, I had *no idea* any of this was going to happen at the house, and that ended up being a special moment for me. I could see the satisfaction in my mother's eyes. It hit me then that my blue couch moment meant as much to my mom as it did to me. That moment wasn't just mine. And all these years later, as a Jesus-loving parent myself, I understand that sentiment.

There were so many emotions for me during that house visit. It is the one and only time there were "ropes" around that couch (or anything in my home). It was the one and only time that anything from my life was presented like a museum. Certainly, the humor of suddenly seeing the place where you grew up turned into an afternoon photo op has never been lost on me (or, I would imagine, on Mom and Dad). But it also hit me that I haven't often taken a step back to view my spiritual history from a distance—that is, until I began writing this book during the first days of lockdown.

The house where my faith was formed was always an open house. It was alive, active, chaotic. When I was growing up, that house was the antithesis of a museum. Museums display history. But that home was where my history was still being written. And that couch where my faith in Jesus first took root was anything but a museum piece. It was lived on, worn, ripped, stained, broken in, and comfortable. The image of that couch roped off is still a good representation in my mind of how my relationship with God felt when I began writing *The God Who Stays*. I had been living as if God was separated from me with those velvet ropes. I had been living a museum kind of faith with a safe distance from God.

Getting My Blue Couch out of the Museum

I absolutely love the movie *Night at the Museum*! It is one of my all-time favorites. I get a kick out of watching the entire museum come to life. Robin Williams is suddenly Teddy Roosevelt on horseback, leading his troops into battle against Attila the Hun.

Owen Wilson is hilarious as Jedediah the cowboy, and Ben Stiller is brilliantly comedic as the incompetent security guard scrambling to save the world. Even the dinosaur bones come to life in the movie. But, outside of that movie, I have to confess that I'm not really the biggest museum guy.

A few years into our marriage, Emily and I took a dream trip to Italy. We rode gondolas in Venice, drank espresso in Florence, and ate our weight in pasta, pastries, and gelato at every stop along the way. The thing about taking a trip to Europe is that it's not really a relaxing experience. It's amazing, but it's exhausting. There is just so much history and too much to see. And it's difficult to shake off the idea that you are on a once-in-a-lifetime trip—"When are we ever going to be back here? We have to see all of these sights now!" Truth be told, if I am given the option between a day at a museum and a fantastic meal at a top-notch restaurant, I'm picking that restaurant every single time. No offense to museum curators; their job is important, but I just get bored. Bored and hungry.

Despite my propensity for boredom, I soldiered on with Emily. I believe that we saw everything that we could see in Italy. There was something different about visiting Rome than the other places I had been before. I was completely captured by so much of the city. The beauty of the Sistine Chapel was overwhelming. But then we arrived at the Holy Stairs, and I simply wasn't prepared for what I witnessed. I literally saw people walking up those stairs weeping and completely overcome with emotion. I've done special events at the Museum of the Bible, which is an amazing place, and as alive as the Scripture can feel in that setting, it still pales in comparison to the experience of seeing biblically significant locations with my own eyes.

Those were the very stairs to the praetorium, or judgment hall, of Pontius Pilate's Jerusalem palace, that Jesus had to climb. Today, those same twenty-eight white marble steps lead to what is called the *Sancta Sanctorum*, which was the first private chapel of the popes. Some believe that Saint Helena, mother of the Roman Emperor Constantine, brought the stairs to Rome after the fourth century. Many visitors choose to ascend those stairs on their knees, praying a different prayer with each step. We learned that believers travel from around the world to climb those stairs together. It was incredible to watch people share the emotion of that moment with one another as they literally walked on the very stones that Jesus walked to His sentencing of crucifixion. I was moved by the aliveness of that moment. A shared faith becomes animated even on the steps of a museum. It was holy.

An Invitation to Stay

And that brings me back again to the blue couch. Of course, I am not comparing that couch to the Holy Stairs. I'm talking about the common space that God shares with us and that we share with others. I guess I haven't really explained one of the most important parts of my blue couch story to you yet. You see, as I watched the Billy Graham sermon that day and felt God speaking to me, I didn't just have that experience by myself.

My mom came and sat on the blue couch and prayed alongside me as I said those first words of commitment to Jesus. My blue couch moment was a *shared* experience. Mom was showing me what it looked like to follow the God who stays by being one of the people who stay. And the lesson is that it doesn't have to be holy staircases in Rome or the Sistine Chapel or even the Baptist church on the corner; God presents blue couch moments anywhere at any moment in our lives. And if we are open and attentive, we can be part of offering those blue couch moments to others. Those experiences aren't meant to be roped off from the world in a time or place or treated like a museum artifact written on a card. They are meant to be shared and carried with us as an invitation to a hurting world.

The journey of this book has reminded me that my faith isn't a museum exhibit. It's not a historic moment in my past where God met me once upon a time. My faith is alive right here and right now. He didn't just stay with me, past tense. He isn't the God who stayed; He is the God who stays, present tense. The God who stays with me and with you. He stays in our joy, our pain, our grief, our sorrow. He stays on mission trips to Haiti, in the cancer ward of children's hospitals, on tour buses, and even in the back of New Jersey cabs. And my blue couch moment is alive and is calling me to clear the space to share the God who stays with everyone I can. Jesus, after sharing space with His disciples, said to them, "A new command I give you: Love one another. As I have loved you, so you must love one another" (John 13:34). Jesus was talking about making room to stay with others. He wasn't asking for some unreachable objective. Just imagine taking the velvet ropes down and inviting others to join you on the blue couch.

"As I have loved you" means that we can't live a roped-off faith. The blue couches of our lives aren't meant to be decorative accessories. And the best couches are always the ones we share with other people. They are a bit lived in, a little worn in, and carry the marks of our tears of grief and joy. I think our blue couches should have spills and stains from shared drinks and breaking bread with others. And let me tell you, what the world needs now more than it ever has are people like you and me, willing to invite others onto our couches to stay. To stay, so that they may rest, cry, pray, grieve, give thanks, and find joy.

Come As You Are to the Blue Couch

My dad was a pastor at the same church for thirty-eight years. When I was a teenager, there were a few times a year when he would attend a regional minister's retreat. I noticed that he never really looked forward to it, and after a while he stopped attending. I asked him about it one time and he explained that the meetings always began with the pastors saying they wanted to create a "safe place" for one another. Where does a minister ever go where they can be ministered to? Having the kind of sheltered environment where they can be accepted and speak freely is a rare situation for pastors.

The gathering was supposed to be a judgment-free zone for them to do what they always encourage their church members to do. It was supposed to be a "come as you are" environment. I told my dad that sounded like a positive thing for those leaders. He said the intentions were good, but the reality was that occasionally, one of the pastors would dare to share candidly about a struggle in his life. But if the problem was deemed a little "too real" for the other leaders, Dad explained, you could physically feel the rest of the room begin to recoil and almost back up from the person who was truly willing to be vulnerable in front of his peers. That story upset me as a teenager. But it also planted a seed somewhere in my mind that grew into the conviction that there are no real safe places. And that is what our blue couches should be for the whole world—a safe place for others to be honest and be themselves, even when things aren't going well.

A Safe Place When Miracles Don't Come Through

We've talked so much in this book about the wilderness experience of these past years. No book is written in a vacuum, and recent history has certainly impacted the way my faith has transformed and grown stronger. It's one thing to witness the pain of the world from a safe distance. It's another thing entirely when the world's heartbreak shows up in your neighborhood. Just like you, I've watched the cruel graphics on every screen of every news channel for months, morbid reminders of the latest death toll from the COVID-19 pandemic. But when my family received the phone call about Jonathan, or "J. O.," as he was known, it suddenly became a harsh reality. You see, J. O.'s daughter is on the cheerleading squad with my oldest daughter, Lulu. He and I are not too far apart in age. We saw each other at games occasionally and shared the joy of being dads to all girls. He was a great guy.

During the spike of the delta variant of COVID-19 in my area of the country, J. O.'s entire family became sick. Each family member bounced back quickly . . . except for J. O. He wound up having to be hospitalized, and the illness took one turn after another for the worse, until the doctors were warning his wife that his chances of survival were not good. That's when my wife's phone rang. It was J. O.'s wife, Julie, and she was asking us to pray. She wondered if we could gather some folks to join with her in prayer. We put the word out, and two hours later a couple hundred people showed up at a nearby church.

I brought my guitar and we sang some worship songs, and then the pastor of the church stood up and began to lead us in prayer. But first, he turned to Julie and simply asked, "What should we be praying for?" She began to cry as she addressed the room. "Honestly, the doctors have done all they can do; I've done all I can do. Now, it's miracle time. We need to pray for a miracle." So, that's exactly what we did. People began to pray out loud, thanking the God who gives sight to the blind and makes the lame walk. The God who stays. "Lord, if it is your will, would you do it again?" I was deeply moved by that prayer time and could feel God working in those sacred, prayer-filled moments. Yes, those too were blue couch moments. It was holy.

I walked out of that church firmly believing that God was

planning a miracle of Lazarus-like proportions. I was hoping the next phone call my wife would receive would be cause for celebration, and that maybe the next time we gathered to worship, J. O. would be one of the grateful voices singing along. But that was not God's plan. At only forty-five years old, our friend's life on earth came to an end. A wife lost her husband, and two daughters lost their dad.

The heart-wrenching pain of loss and grief has moved into so many of our neighborhoods, and in our lifetimes we will all know what it's like to lose someone we love.

Hurry Up and Heal?

As the days progressed, I thought about what happens to our grieving friends when the funeral is over and the news cycles have shifted. What happens when everyone has moved on with their busy lives and people aren't checking in quite as often. The meals from neighbors have slowed and the cards stop coming. It must feel like the world is back to normal, while you're just getting started with the firsts. The first anniversary without him. The first birthday when she's not there. The first Christmas. The kind of firsts that usher in wave upon wave of grief and loneliness, loss, and fear. And who stays with them? Who is offering a seat on the blue couch for them?

I know one woman who tragically lost her teenage son in a car accident. At first, she said, her friends were supportive and vowed to walk with her through her grieving. But after months and months of hard days, she felt her support system waning. One friend even had the nerve to tell her, "It's time to move on." Wow. Telling someone it's time to move on is the equivalent of saying, "Hurry up and heal." It brings me comfort to read about the God who is "close to the brokenhearted," as Psalm 34:18 says. I've told you how my dad and I sit there on Wednesday mornings and see thousands of prayer requests rolling in. Most of the time we can say a quick prayer at best for them. But who is there to stay for those requests? Who is offering those hurting people a blue couch invitation?

What You Did for These People

Thankfully, the God who stays doesn't say "hurry up and heal." Instead, He says, "I'm never going to leave you or forsake you." God doesn't say, "Get your act together or I'm leaving!" He doesn't tell you to get over your depression. He doesn't get impatient with your grief. He doesn't get scared away by your anger. He stays. He stays when the miracle doesn't happen the way you thought it should. He stays when the dream comes to an end. And He says things like, "Matthew, climb down from that sycamore tree and let's have dinner. Come sit with me on the blue couch." He offers Himself to every situation we can possibly face. His answer is always His presence, and that is the beauty of being the people of God who are loved by God, isn't it? That we also offer ourselves in the same way.

Jesus said, "Whatever you did for one of the least of

these . . . you did for me" (Matt. 25:40, my paraphrase). He stays with us in all our pain and suffering, in all our joy and laughter, just as we are—and in the same way, we are called to stay with others. How can we respond to the love of God and be the people who stay for others? I'm talking about being the people who *really* stay—who stay after the rest of the world moves on. Who can have the patience and compassion to walk somebody's broken road with them, even if the steps are slow and heavy. Who can sit through the hard questions. Can we stay even when the story is messy? Even as God has stayed for us?

And that is just the thing—the blue couch moment isn't transactional. You don't often sit down with people on a couch to do business. They've got conference tables for that sort of thing. You don't stay for what you receive. It's a place of rest, of transformation and connection. When you sit on the couch in your home, your guard comes down. It is a safe place where you open your life to relationship. I think that is what Jesus wants your whole life to look like. Offering a safe place for others in *your* space. After all, that is how Jesus lived. That is what He offers to you. He was a safe place for the woman at the well. Jesus was a safe place for lepers. Jesus was a safe place for social outcasts. He was a safe place for the sick. Jesus was a safe place for foreigners. I think the question I am asking myself these days is, How can I be a safe place for someone to let their own truth be told? How can I create space for them on my blue couch? And how can I help someone else discover their own blue couch moments?

Inviting Others to Their Moments with God

The more I grow in my awareness of the closeness of God in my life and His nearness to my heart, the more I want to offer the same *safety*, *rest*, and *honesty* to others. I want them to come to know the Lord and experience the joy of His life-changing presence in their lives. Isn't that the ultimate calling for all of us who have experienced the faithfulness of the God who stays? And the image of the blue couch as that kind of invitation has even moved into my podcast and taught me so much about creating space for others in my life to share their experiences. I have a segment on each podcast now where I ask my guest to talk about their own blue couch moment. It is a way of opening the conversation about what God is doing in our lives. Most of the time that part of the conversation gets real. It's a shared space, and it is holy.

I had an interview with a good friend of mine named Jon who was the former front man for a Christian band. Not just any band—it was one of the most popular Christian bands in the world. They had a ton of radio hits and toured the world sharing the good news about Jesus. We had the chance to share the stage together on many occasions. Jon is a preacher's kid just like me. But he publicly announced a few years ago that he no longer believes in God. Of all the people I've asked to share about their blue couch story with me, Jon's answer was the most heartbreaking but also the most hopeful at the same time. His answer was, "I'm asking God for that moment now, and I don't feel like I've had it, and if He's there, I want it. When I pray, that's what I'm asking for; I'm asking for a blue couch moment."

I see the blue couch now not just as a representation of God's presence but as a reminder, a call to invite people to sit with me, to create a space for them to stay so that they can rest, cry, pray, grieve, give thanks, find joy, and hopefully find the God who stays with them. Remember, the couch is a gathering space where life takes place—there isn't six feet of separation from your community on a couch. As we emerge from a season of physical distancing, and for many (myself included) a season of spiritual distancing, I think God is calling you to make room for other people. God stays and He is calling us to be a people who stay for the moments when there are no words but to cry out for His presence. I can still remember the feel of those Story House piano keys as I first found the tune:

You're the God who stands
With wide open arms
And You tell me nothing I have ever done can separate my heart
From the God who stays

I guess the blue couch has become a reminder to me that I am to live as a reflection of a God who moves with me through every season of life. I want my life to be a light shining on a hill and an invitation into a story of love, joy, peace, endurance, kindness, goodness, faithfulness, gentleness, and self-control. I want to live in a way that welcomes people to sit down and stay awhile with me there. When I imagine God walking with me in the garden in the cool of the day like He did with Adam and Eve, I wonder if He wouldn't just rather sit down with me for a talk on an old blue couch with all its lived-in rips, tears, stains, and slouchy cushions—maybe even with one of my favorite old gospel hymns like "Just As I Am" playing somewhere in the background. "Just as I am without one plea, but that thy blood was shed for me."[1]

The words that grew out of my love for old hymns highlight God's challenge for us to be "people who stay." You see, God invited me to that first blue couch moment just as I was. There were no prerequisites, no regulations, no secret handshakes, and no steps of progress necessary to prove myself worthy of His blue couch moment for me. And every day God invites you and me again to come to Him . . . just as we are. I think that's exactly the kind of invitation God wants us to share.

I wonder if we can be brave enough to allow God through the roped-off areas of our faith that need to come down today. Can we allow Him to breathe life back into the places of our hearts that have become like museums of faith? I wonder if Jesus is simply waiting on you to extend an invitation for people to experience their own blue couch moments . . . just as they are. Can we be there for the hurting, wounded, sick, or lost who are just waiting for that one person to offer them a place to rest? I pray that we can live a life of faith that always makes room on the blue couch to share the good news of the God who stays. May we always be the people who stay for a broken and hurting world.

Notes

Chapter 2: Why Does God Stay?

1. C. Austin Miles, "In the Garden," 1913, in *Baptist Hymnal* (Nashville: Convention Press, 1991), 187, Hymnary.org, https://hymnary.org/text/i_come_to_the_garden_alone.

Chapter 5: God Stays Out of Safe Spaces

1. Frederick Buechner, *Beyond Words: Daily Readings in the ABC's of Faith* (New York: HarperCollins, 2004), 139.
2. Bethany Hamilton, "About" page, Bethany (blog), accessed March 11, 2022, https://bethanyhamilton.com/about/.

Chapter 6: God Stays with Those in Need

1. Mother Teresa (lecture, Norwegian Nobel Committee, Oslo, Norway, December 10, 1979). See "Acceptance Speech," NobelPrize.org, accessed March 11, 2022, https://www.nobelprize.org/prizes/peace/1979/teresa/acceptance-speech/.

Chapter 7: God Stays in Times of Anxiety and Fear

1. Jaime McLeod, "Remembering the Perfect Storm: The 1991 Halloween Nor'easter," *Farmers' Almanac*, updated October 25, 2021, https://www.farmersalmanac.com/remembering-the-perfect-storm-3314.
2. "Understand Anxiety & Depresssion," Anxiety and Depression

Association of America, accessed September 19, 2021, https://adaa.org/understanding-anxiety/facts-statistics.

3. Brianna Ehley, "CDC: One Quarter of Young Adults Contemplated Suicide During Pandemic," Politico, August 13, 2020, https://www.politico.com/news/2020/08/13/cdc-mental-health-pandemic-394832.

4. "He's Got the Whole World in His Hands," in *Baptist Hymnal* (Nashville: Convention Press, 1991), 346, Hymnary.org, https://hymnary.org/text/hes_got_the_whole_world_in_his_hands.

Chapter 8: God Stays for the Party

1. Henry Van Dyke, "Joyful, Joyful, We Adore Thee," 1907, in *Baptist Hymnal* (Nashville: Convention Press, 1991), 7, Hymnary.org, https://hymnary.org/text/joyful_joyful_we_adore_thee.

2. George W. Cooke, "Joy in My Heart," 1926, in *African American Heritage Hymnal* (Chicago: GIA Publications, 2001), 622, Hymnary.org, https://hymnary.org/text/i_have_the_joy_joy_joy_joy_down_in_my_h.

Chapter 10: God Stays the Same

1. C. S. Lewis, *The Lion, the Witch, and the Wardrobe* (1950; repr., New York: HarperCollins, 2000).

2. Edward Mote, "My Hope Is Built on Nothing Less," 1834, in *Baptist Hymnal* (Nashville: Convention Press, 1991), 406, Hymnary.org, https://hymnary.org/text/my_hope_is_built_on_nothing_less.

3. Brennan Manning, *The Ragamuffin Gospel* (1990; repr., Colorado Springs: Multnomah, 2005), 14.

4. "My Hope Is Built on Nothing Less," 1834, in *Baptist Hymnal* (Nashville: Convention Press, 1991), 406, Hymnary.org, https://hymnary.org/text/my_hope_is_built_on_nothing_less

Chapter 11: Being the People Who Stay

1. Charlotte Elliott, "Just As I Am," 1835, in *Baptist Hymnal* (Nashville: Convention Press, 1991), 307, Hymnary.org, https://hymnary.org/text/just_as_i_am_without_one_plea.

Acknowledgments

Thank you . . .

Emily, Lulu, and Delaney. You'll go down in history as my greatest hits. To my mom and dad who believed someday I would be writing songs and books about Jesus. You were right!

Matt Litton for lending your incredible gift to these pages.

Thanks to all of my popwe ministry supporters.

To Kyle Olund and the staff at W. Publishing, Steve Green, Story House Collective, Crowd Surf, and the entire team who has worked tirelessly to get the book out into the world.

Thank you, God, for the life changing gift of Your presence. I pray that everyone who picks up this book will discover that You truly are the God who stays.

–mw

About the Author

MATTHEW WEST is a five-time Grammy nominee, a multiple ASCAP Christian Music Songwriter/Artist of the Year winner, and a 2018 Dove Award Songwriter of the Year (Artist) recipient. He has received an American Music Award, a Billboard Music Award, and a K-LOVE Fan Award and was named Billboard's Hot Christian Songwriter of the Year. He has cohosted the K-LOVE Fan Awards numerous times and has more than 130 songwriting credits to his name, including cuts by Rascal Flatts, Scotty McCreery, Michael W. Smith, Amy Grant, Mandisa, Danny Gokey, and Casting Crowns.

Matthew is the host of the popular weekly podcast *The Matthew West Podcast*, with more than one million listeners so far. He has written six books to date: *Give This Christmas Away*; *The Story of Your Life*; *Forgiveness*; *Today Is Day One*; *Hello, My Name Is*; and now his latest, *The God Who Stays*. He is also passionate about providing hope and healing through the power of prayer and story. Along with his father, Pastor Joe West, they founded popwe, a nonprofit ministry helping others craft, share, and live a more meaningful life. Matthew and his wife, Emily, live in Nashville with their two daughters, Lulu and Delaney, and their dog, Nick.

MATT LITTON is a bestselling collaborative writer, developmental editor, and writing coach. He is the author of *The Mockingbird Parables* (Tyndale), *Holy Nomad* (Abingdon Press), and *In the Presence of Jesus* (Tyndale). He resides in Nashville, Tennessee.

Every life has a story to tell. The vision of
pop**we** is to share the hope of Jesus Christ to
every person, no matter how broken, and see
their life's story changed by the power of God.

Our stories stem from God actively working in our lives
every day. pop**we** provides resources, prayer support, and
weekly devotions to enable our community to see God's
grace at work and accompany them on their journey of
discovery and healing.

A MATTHEW WEST MINISTRY

Scan QR code and sign up to receive **free** weekly devotions from Matthew!

pop**we**.org